"NEW MASS" CONCLUSIVELY INVALID

According to the Preponderance of Evidence

by

Fr. Paul Trinchard, S.T.L.

Published by

MAETA
METAIRIE LOUISIANA

Published by MAETA

Printed in the United States of America

ISBN: 1-889168-28-9

Library of Congress Control Number: 2004108410

MAETA
P. O. BOX 6012
METAIRIE LA 70009-6012

Dedicated and entrusted to the Most Sacred Heart of Jesus Who instituted and "enlivens" the Canonized Latin Mass text; to Our Lady of the Canonized Mass; to the priest-saint of the Canonized Latin Mass–St. Padre Pio, who refused to celebrate "New Mass," and who prayed and lived the Canonized Latin Mass so as to become the only priest-saint of the Latin Patriarchate to receive the stigmata.

In a special way, dedicated to Pope Leo XIII ((1878-1903) who prophesied liturgical apostasy; (See his Leonine Prayer.) and defended the essentials of Catholicism in his encyclical, *Apostolicae Curae, On the Nullity of Anglican Orders,* pronouncing theAnglican Ordinal and "New Mass" *null and void,"* not valid.

Pope Leo XIII decreed the nullity of Anglican Orders, *Apostolicae Curae*, on Sept. 13, 1896. The principles he used to evaluate the validity of the Anglican Ordinal, and, consequently, its services, are the same used in this book to evaluate the Bishops' "New Mass."

TABLE OF CONTENTS

Part One

HISTORY OF CHRIST'S CANONIZED LATIN MASS AND OF "NEW MASS"

TABLE OF CONTENTS

Part Two

EVALUATING THE "NEW MASS"

TABLE OF CONTENTS

Part Three

THE NATURE OR PURPOSE OF "NEW MASS"

About the Author

Fr. Paul Trinchard was ordained as a Jesuit on June 7, 1966. He is now a retired diocesan priest. He has a Masters degree in philosophy and in physics and has studied the philosophy of science at San Francisco State, Columbia University, American University and Hebrew University. He also earned a pontifical Licentiate in Sacred Theology, specializing in Paul Tillich.

It is interesting to note that Fr. Trinchard began to pray the Canonized Mass upon his retirement in 1989. As he prayed and studied, Fr. Trinchard began to write his books on the Mass, and has written 15 books since his conversion.

Major endorsement for his exegesis of the Canonized Latin Mass prayers has come from "several officials in the Roman congregation" (See Malachi Martin's letter.); and, also, from a holy archbishop, highly dedicated to the Canonized Latin Liturgy. It is our prayer that this book may be instrumental in leading bishops and other clerics to "an appreciation of" and "conversion to" the Canonized Latin Mass.

Editor's Note:

In 1996, Rev. Dr. Malachi Martin reviewed Fr. Trinchard's exegesis of the Canonized Latin Mass Prayers for the Ordinary of the Mass. The following are his remarks.

> **As more and more of the Catholic laity return to attendance at the immemorial Latin Mass, there is a felt need for a vernacular translation which is accurate and reverential. Fr. Trinchard's exegesis of the Missal meets this need. No greater praise can be given of this work than to say that Pope St. Gregory the Great who codified our beautiful Mass in the 6th century, would have been wholly enthusiastic for this translation–its grace, accuracy, prayerfulness. I have shown it to several officials in the Roman congregation. They singly praise it highly.**

†Malachi Martin
(R.I.P.)

THE LEONINE PRAYER

1930 Official Edition 300 days once a day Pope Leo XIII

O Glorious Archangel St. Michael, Prince of the heavenly Host, be our defence in the terrible warfare which we carry on against Principalities and Powers, against the rulers of this world of darkness, spirits of evil. Come to the aid of man, whom God created immortal, made in His own image and likeness, and redeemed at a great price from the tyranny of the devil.

Fight this day the battle of the Lord, together with the holy angels, as already thou hast fought the leader of the proud angels, Lucifer, and his apostate host, who were powerless to resist thee, nor was there place for them any longer in Heaven. That cruel, that ancient serpent who is called the devil or Satan, who seduces the whole world, was cast into the abyss with his angels.

Behold, this primeval enemy and slayer of men has taken courage. Transformed into an angel of light, he wanders about with all the multitude of wicked spirits, invading the earth in order to blot out the name of God and of his Christ, to seize upon, slay and cast into eternal perdition, souls destined for the crown of eternal glory.

This wicked dragon pours out, as a most impure flood, the venom of his malice on men of depraved mind and corrupt heart, the spirit of lying, of impiety, of blasphemy and the pestilent breath of impurity, and of every vice and iniquity.

These most crafty enemies have filled and inebriated with gall and bitterness the Church, the spouse of the immaculate Lamb, and have laid impious hands on her most sacred possessions.

In the holy place itself, where has been set up the See of the Most Holy Peter and the Chair of Truth for the light of the world, they have raised the throne of their abominable impiety, with the iniquitous design that when the pastor has been struck, the sheep may be scattered.

Arise then, O invincible prince, bring help against the attacks of the lost spirits to the people of God, and give them the victory. They venerate thee as their protector and patron; in thee, holy Church glories as her defence against the malicious power of hell; to thee has God entrusted the souls of men to be established in heavenly beatitude.

Oh, pray to the God of peace that He may put Satan under our feet, so far conquered that he may no longer be able to hold men in captivity and harm the Church. Offer our prayers in the sight of the Most High, so that they may quickly conciliate the mercies of the Lord; and beating down the dragon, the ancient serpent, who is the devil and Satan, do thou again make him captive in the abyss, that he may no longer seduce the nations. Amen.

Behold, the Cross of the Lord; Be scattered ye hostile powers. The Lion of the tribe of Juda has conquered, the root of David. Let Thy mercies be upon us, O Lord, as we have hoped in Thee. O Lord, hear my prayer, and let my cry come unto Thee.

Let us pray. O God the Father of Our Lord Jesus Christ, we call upon Thy Holy Name; and as supplicants, we implore Thy clemency, that by the intercession of Mary, ever Virgin Immaculate and our Mother, and of the glorious Archangel St. Michael, Thou wouldst deign to help us against Satan and all other unclean spirits who wander the world for the injury of the human race and the ruin of souls. Amen.

PART ONE

HISTORY OF CHRIST'S CANONIZED LATIN MASS AND OF "NEW MASS"

Ill. 21—Old Drawing of the Vanished Mosaic of Ricimer in the Church of S. Agata dei Goti at Rome

"To the Catholic, who realized all that the Mass meant, how it was the center of his religion and the sublime Christ-bestowed Sacrifice–it was a point of honor and conscience to imperil fortune and even life itself for so sacred heritage."

(Cardinal) Abbot Gasquet, 1913. Author of *Apostolicae Curae,* which condemned the New Anglican Order

Christ instituted the Mass; His Church Canonized the Mass to be "as He instituted" in perpetuity–forever–period! As regards the Bishops' "New Mass," Pope Paul VI's own words refer to "New Mass" as a "novelty." The plenitude of the constant teaching of the Catholic Church (only a fraction of which appears in these pages) constitutes the preponderance of evidence which leads one to conclude that "New Mass" cannot be valid. This book does not reflect evidence as in a court case, but rather, brings to the fore, truths of the Christ-instituted Holy Mass and Catholic Church and the mandate from Christ to uphold (but never change) Christ-given Salutary Truth.

"When the new Mass was finally presented to Pope Paul VI, he ordered the General Instruction for the Mass to be submitted to the Congregation for the Doctrine of the Faith for examination and approval. In an act of unprecedented disobedience, the Secretary of the Liturgy Commission which had prepared the new Mass ignored the Pope's request and had it printed. When Pope Paul found out, he wept, from sorrow, shame and anger, said one cardinal."

Leo Darroch, Deputy Chairman of the Latin Mass Society of England and Wales, lecture, May 3, 1995, www.latin-mass-society.org/leomass.htm p 6 &7

"A new Mass was first celebrated in public in the Sistine Chapel on 24th October 1967 before the Synod of Bishops. Afterwards, many of the bishops were very uneasy about what they had seen. Only 71 out of a total of 176 voted 'Yes'for the new rite. The rest voted 'No' or had reservations. It must also be remembered that the rest of the world's bishops were not given the opportunity of voting. The fact that their new rite of Mass had been rejected did not deter the reformers because this, in fact, with very minor alterations, became your new Mass."

Leo Darroch, Deputy Chairman of the Latin Mass Society of England and Wales, lecture, May 3, 1995, www.latin-mass-society.org/leomass.htm p 6

Chapter One

FOUNTAINHEADS OF EVIL REFLECTED WITHIN "NEW MASS"

According to Pope Paul VI, "New Mass" is a liturgical "novelty." As such, it constitutes "abominable impiety" and is the source of a "new religion."

"Catholics" now dwell within the religion of "New Mass." This "New Mass" is the *abominable impiety* predicted by Pope Leo XIII in his prayer soliciting the help of St. Michael to protect us from that [existential]church which will have *"raised its throne of abominable impiety* [the 'New Mass']... ***in the holy place itself...the See of the Most Holy Peter."* Pope Leo XIII predicted that, in the end times, abominable impiety, the "New Mass" will proceed from Rome.**

The "New Mass" has poisoned Christ's existential church. Liturgizing and, thus, believing in the poison of "New Mass" provokes and promotes other poisoned fountainheads of evil. If man, "replaces God" at "New Mass," then, in effect, he becomes the primary consideration in other areas of religion as well. [This is the law of *lex orandi, lex credendi* - one's prayer determines one's belief.]

The Sacrament of Matrimony Poisoned

In a sacrilege, we find a special type of deformation, namely, the violation of a sacred thing by treating it with irreverence.

St. Thomas Aquinas, Summa Th., II, Q. 99, Art. 2

The Bishops' "New Mass" poisoned and radically deformed the sacred and the Most Holy, both as referring to sources of life or "roots" and as implying a total or major deformation (or poisoning). [It did so to the extent that clergy and laity alike began to say that a whole "new religion " came into being and that "all that came before" was now subject to revision or "new thought."] Sacrilegiously, they redefined words in order to give a whole new meaning.

One shining example of such a major deformation affecting the Sacrament of Matrimony is the Bishops' sexual abuse of children by sex education and indoctrination (in "religion" class). This subject would take us too far afield other than to explain that the Church has never approved sex education, always insisting on moral education. The Bishops' sex education (which cannot be avoided in alleged "Catholic" schools even if parents object) affects Matrimony because it redefines man from "a

creature composed of body and soul and made into the image and likeness of God (Baltimore Catechism)**" to "a sexual creature from birth until death** (sex ed manuals)**."**

Does not this very definition imply that sex is as natural a process as breathing and must be engaged in? Saturated with sex information from kindergarten up (including how to achieve orgasms and how to avoid pregnancy) is it any surprise that this has resulted in an avalanche of divorces, giving the Bishops an excuse to devise "new matrimony"-- "a covenant of life and love?"(as defined in canons 1055 & 1098, 1983 Code of Canon Law)**.**

In diocesan tribunals, any failure to establish a covenant of life and love annuls a marriage. To grant "annulments," this definition or principle is applied *retroactively*. In a typical application, a couple divorced and remarried civilly, "must have failed" to establish a covenant of life and love or marriage: the original couple (s) had failed to be married–i.e., had failed to establish covenant (s) of life and love. Therefore, they were free to try again (to do the impossible).

To the credit of Pope John Paul II, it must be admitted that he perceived the "Catholic divorce problem" correctly. Yet, he was ineffective in his protestations because he failed to perceive that man-made "New

Mass" fosters a selfish new man-made religion (alien to Catholicism), which defines Matrimony, not as Christ instituted it, but in a more user-friendly manner, like the "New Mass" -- disobedient to God, but more suitable to man. "New Mass" begat "new spirituality" which begat "new religion" which begat "new sex ed;" which begat "new matrimony" which begat "new wholesale granting of annulments" or "new 'Catholic' divorces;" etc. to a "new infinity." In opposition to the Bishops' "new matrimony," Catholicism holds:

> **1) that marriage is the exchange to the use of the other's body for the sake of procreation;**
>
> **2) that marriage is until death, both for the sake of raising children (if any) and for the sake of the other party;**
>
> **3) marriage exists to *allay concupiscence.* We note, in passing, that even the "third aspect" of "allay" as in the old Webster Dictionary, is to "put down or suppress." (See MAETA's *Matrimony the Sacrament.*)**

These fountainheads of evil demonstrate the "law of prayer and the law of belief." Praying an alien "New Mass" has brought forth a selfish new and alien religion. G.K. Chesterton had forecast that *"the next great heresy would be a cult of sex"* **[*The Chesterton Review,* Vol. No. 1, Feb. 1987, p. 48, E.J. Oliver, quoting Chesterton (1874-1936) in an article entitled, "Chesterton and Primitive Religion." Mothers' Watch, Spring 2004, POB 1029, Frederick MD 21702-0029].**

"That Chesterton used the word 'cult' is important considering the obstinate, self-righteous contempt with which parents are treated by Bishops, priests and diocesan educators. Those drawn into cults are recognized by their own narrow beliefs and their resistance to reason or rational argument and their absolute intolerance of opposite views.

When Bishops, priests and diocesan educators refuse to listen to parents who, with arms full of proof, protest classroom sex programs, it is time to recognize this great evil that has befallen our Church and do something about it." **Mothers' Watch, Spring 2004,** (1-410-761-7437)

No More – "Obey and Trust Us!"

This book has a greater chance of being accepted, having been written after the press exposed "homosexual-promoting bishops." Fr. Rueda's book *(The Homosexual Network)* was written several decades before the "episcopal homosexual expose`." In general, its facts and reasoning were rejected. The time was not ripe. Bishops were still blindly (and "blindingly") trusted, obeyed, and reverenced.

However, the time is now ripe. Surveys in 2004 prove that people have discarded their blinding

trustfulness of Bishops. Studies show that over 80% are convinced that the present sex-problem originates from and was advanced by the Bishops. They want Bishops to "`fess up," resign and be punished for actively sponsoring and promoting a homosexual clergy (from the sixties on).

However, what Bishops did in this area is as nothing compared to their gross violation of Catholics by forcing "their" flocks to attend anti-Catholic, anti-Christ, sacrilegious and invalid Mass simulations – gross, "soul-damning" mockeries of the Most Sacred. Freed from the bondage of establishment propaganda, "let yourself" see and confess the awful truth: "New Mass" is conclusively invalid (as well as, sacrilegious and demonic).

"When good priests in obedience to their bishops, will have sufficiently distanced themselves from what is divine and lost themselves in what is human, come to realize that they have been 'had,' it will be too late...Here is the episcopal crime committed against the Priesthood."

Abbe de Nantes, Ccr, n 25, p.9

Chapter Two

CHRIST-GIVEN CANONIZED LATIN MASS TEXT: OF FAITH AND OF HISTORY

"Our Mass [the Canonized Latin Mass Text] **goes back without significant change to the age when Caesar ruled the world and thought he could stamp out the faith of Christ."** Fr. Adrian Fortescue, foremost English historian

~~~~~~~~~~~~ **Canonized Latin Mass Text** ~~~~~~~~~~~~

From: *Suscipe, sancte Pater, omnipotens aeterne Deus, hanc immaculatam hostiam, quam ego indignus famuluis tuus offero tibi Deo meo vivo et vero pro innumerabilibus peccatis, et offensionibus, et negligentiis meis, et pro omnibus circumstantibus, sed it pro omnibus fidelibus christianis vivis atque defunctis: ut mihi, et illis proficiat ad salutem in vitam aeternam. Amen.* ... .
Through: ... *Per ip ✠ sum, et cum ip ✠ so, et in ip ✠ so, est tibi Deo Patri ✠ omnipotenti, in unitate Spiritus ✠ Sancti, omnis honor et gloria.*

~~~~~~

It is dogmatic Catholic belief and irrefutable historical fact that the "essential Canonized Latin Mass Text" was given by Christ to His Apostles (after the resurrection and before His ascension); kept intact; and thus, was, is, and will always be, canonized by the *sensus et praxis fidelium* from Apostolic times until the end of time. Today's Canonized Latin Mass Text was instituted by Christ and is the same Mass used from Apostolic times. No solid historical evidence disproves or calls into doubt this "fundamental truth" and this basic essential belief of the Catholic Faith. This Mass Text from

Christ "used by the Apostles." constitutes and establishes the Sacred Tradition of the Church.

As regards historical confirmation, it is providentially miraculous that Christ's Canonized Latin Mass Prayers (the essential Mass prayers of the priest from the Offertory through the Communion) are found in reliable documents originating from the time of St. Gregory the Great (600 A.D.). This Mass Liturgy irrevocably defines Christ's Canonized Latin Mass Prayers for the Latin Rite until the end of time.

Previous to 600 A.D., there exist exegetical extracts from Justin and a few others which are not "Mass texts;" nor, are they reliable exegeses. *De facto,* they come to us as "broken-off, unauthenticated fragments or exegesis of the Canonized Latin Mass. Despite rejection as "Mass" texts, by the early Church, these were "resurrected as Mass texts" in order to establish the "theory of Mass evolution."

A few latter-day, research speculators claim to be more reliable than the Church Fathers who were then alive and helped form (through Christ) the Tradition of the Church. Using "excerpts," they postulate a "theory of Mass-evolution," that "churches of each period of history and each locale are infallible" because of living apostolic authority"

(their heretical belief that Bishops of each and every "place and time" in history are "living apostles," and, as such, can "undo" or negate binding Apostolic Tradition. Regardless of this false theory, ***such alleged Mass "excerpts" coming to us from before the 5th century are not authentic nor reliable Mass texts.*** **They cannot be used to establish the "evolution of Mass."**

The Canonized Bible Texts and Canonized Mass Texts are two noticeable exceptions to the general rule of "ancient historical unreliability." Both of these: 1) the Holy Bible (being respected as the Word of God); and 2) Mass Texts (being the Christ-instituted "formula" to bring about the Realization of God's Saving Will on earth as it is in Heaven); constitute Apostolic Tradition.

Christ's Canonized Mass Liturgy is of its very nature to be kept "secret and inviolably intact," since it is the most important relevant "faith datum" and "faith essential" entrusted to His Church as its defining element. ***These essentials of the one and only Christ-instituted Mass and religion were studiously protected from "internal and external profanation" by the (faithful to Apostolic Tradition) "priestly class,"*** **according to the dogmatic teaching of the Church, latter-day nay-sayers notwithstanding.**

Historical Truths and History of the Canonized Latin Mass

"In the Catholic Church Herself, every care must be taken that we may hold fast to that which has been believed everywhere, always and by all. For this is truly and properly Catholic." St. Vincent Lerins 450 A.D.

The following time-dated highlights confirm the continuity of our liturgical past from Apostolic times to 1962, the Bishops' Revolt. Papal confirmations highlight the ever-binding and immutable dogma of Christ's Canonized Latin Mass Liturgy as being the one and only acceptable, spiritually profitable (and, thereby, the only) valid liturgy for the Latin Rite.

88 A.D.: In his letter to the Corinthians Pope St. Clement of Rome professed that our Lord gave us the Mass in its principle parts: Offertory, Consecration and Communion.

155 A.D.: St. Justin attested to the fact that the Mass was taught to Christ's Apostles by the Resurrected Christ. The Canonized Latin Mass, like unto the sacraments, was instituted by Christ.

360 A.D.: St. Ambrose, in *De Sacramentis,* wrote down "exegeses or commentaries on Mass prayers"

of the Latin or Roman Rite. [Modern, biased, anti-Christ, anti-Church "research" heretics (in defiance of Church-proclaimed disallowance of such as Mass texts) bring forth these "shadowy fragments" in order to impose upon the faithful their heretical, historically inaccurate, manmade theory that "Mass evolved" and continues "to evolve."]

600 A.D.: Pope St. Gregory the Great (by his papal dogmatization *in praxis*) reaffirms the canonization of Christ's Latin Mass Text which had been canonized by the *sensus et praxis fidelium* over the past 560 or so years. [This very same Latin Rite Mass Ritual and Text (which is the focus of our attention) would be "explicitly and officially word for word" irreformably and forever frozen as being canonical by the dogmatic Council of Trent, through the dogmatic *Quo Primum.]* This Text and Ritual (and "no other text or ritual") forever defines Christ's Canonized Latin Mass for the Latin Rite. For our purposes, the Canonized Text of this Canonized Latin Mass is defined by the *"Suscipe Sancte Pater..."* through the *"Per Ipsum"* prayers.

1570 A.D.: The dogmatic Council of Trent and *Quo Primum* (Pope Saint Pius V) irrevocably and precisely canonized (word for word) the Canonized Latin Mass ceremonies and prayers of the Latin Rite

from *"Suscipe Sancte Pater..."* through *"Per Ipsum..."* plus the necessity of the priest's communion.

Quo Primum

Specifically, do we warn all persons in authority of whatever dignity or rank, and command them as a matter of strict obedience never to use or permit any ceremonies or Mass prayers other than the ones contained in this Missal...

At no time in the future can a priest, whether secular or order priest, ever be forced to use any other way of saying Mass. And in order once and for all to preclude any scruples of conscience and fear of ecclesiastical penalties and censures, we declare herewith that it is by virtue of our Apostolic authority that we decree and prescribe that this present order and decree of ours is to last in perpetuity, and never at a future date can it be revoked or amended legally...

And if, nevertheless, anyone would dare attempt any action contrary to this order of ours, handed down for all times, let him know that he has incurred the wrath of Almighty God and of the Blessed Apostles Peter and Paul.

Pope Pius V, *Quo Primum,* 1570

1896 A.D.: Pope Leo XIII declared Anglican orders and services to be "null and void" in his encyclical, *Apostolicae Curae.* (Sept.13, 1896). Pope Leo's prayer (as

quoted in its entirety in the front of this book) clearly predicts, warns against and prays to prevent "abominable impiety," or the "New Mass."

Apostolicae Curae
(On the Nullity of Anglican Orders)

We have...maintained that...in England, shortly after it was rent from the center of Christian Unity, a new rite for conferring Holy Orders was publicly introduced... the true Sacrament of Order as instituted by Christ lapsed, and with it the hierarchical succession...in these last years especially, a controversy has sprung up as to whether the Sacred Orders conferred according to the Edwardine Ordinal possessed the nature and effect of a Sacrament...

It is necessary to lay down a fundamental principle...not intended to deal with an abstract state...but with a specific and concrete issue...For it is clearly and definitely noted that there were two classes of men; the first...who had really received Holy Orders, either before Henry VIII, or if after it, and by ministers infected by error and schism, still according to the accustomed Catholic rite; the second, those who were initiated according to the Edwardine Ordinal, who on that account could not be "promoted," since they had received an ordination which was null....Paul IV issued his bull *Praeclara Charissimi* of that same year.

Being fully cognizant of the necessary connection between faith and worship, between "the law of believing and the law of praying," under a pretext of returning to the primitive

form, they corrupted the Liturgical Order in many ways to suit the errors of the reformers. For this reason, in the whole Ordinal, not only is there no clear mention of the sacrifice, of consecration, of the priesthood (sacerdotium) and of the power of consecrating and offering sacrifice, as we have just stated. Every trace of these things which had been in such prayers of the Catholic rite as had not entirely been rejected, was deliberately removed and struck out.

Pope Leo XIII, 1896

1907 A.D.: Underlining the primary and essential duty of all priests (especially, popes and bishops) to preserve, apply and transmit intact to the next generation, all significant elements of Catholic Faith and Morals (especially, the Sacred Heart of Catholicism, the Christ-instituted word-for-word Canonized Latin Mass Prayers). Pope St. Pius X warns future popes and bishops of the demonic spirit of modernism (which would develop into the evil disobedient spirit of Vatican Two); issuing his dogmatic encyclical, *Pascendi Dominici Gregis* (On Caring for the Lord's Flock); and mandates his clergy to take the Oath Against Modernism. To put "teeth into" his encyclical, *Pascendi Dominici Gregis,* and to emphasize the importance and necessity of handing down the Faith intact; in its clear, obvious and literal meaning,[in other words, to prevent the birth of "New Mass" and a "new religion" in his day] Pope St. Pius X required the clergy; and, specifically,

every candidate to the priesthood, to take the following *Oath Against Modernism*.

> **"I most firmly hold, and will hold until my dying breath, the Faith of the Fathers on the certain rule of truth...and I hold it not withstanding that a thing can be held which seems better and more suited to the culture of a particular age, but I hold it in such a way that *"nothing else is to be believed by the words;* and I hold that this absolute and unchangeable truth preached by the Apostles from the earliest times is to be understood *in no other way than by the words."***
>
> **Oath Against Modernism, in use until 1966 (or the episcopal imposition of the New Mass)**

Pascendi Dominici Gregis
On Caring for the Lord's Flock

1. One of the primary obligations assigned by Christ to the office divinely committed to Us of feeding the Lord's flock is that of guarding with the greatest vigilance the deposit of the faith delivered to the saints, rejecting the profane novelties of words and the gainsaying of knowledge falsely so called. There has never been a time when this watchfulness of the supreme pastor was not necessary to the Catholic body, for owing to the efforts of the enemy of the human race, there have never been lacking "men speaking perverse things," "vain talkers and seducers," "erring and driving into error." It must, however, be confessed that these latter days have witnessed a notable increase in the number of the enemies of the Cross of Christ, who, by arts entirely new and full of deceit, are striving to

destroy the vital energy of the Church, its "soul"and, as far as in them lies, utterly to subvert the very Kingdom of Christ. Wherefore, We may no longer keep silence, lest We should seem to fail in Our most sacred duty, and lest the kindness that, in the hope of wiser counsels, We have hitherto shown them, should be set down to lack of diligence in the discharge of Our office.

2. That We should act without delay in this matter is made imperative especially by the fact that the partisans of error are to be sought not only among the Church's open enemies; but, what is to be most dreaded and deplored, in her very bosom.

Pascendi Dominici Gregis, Pope St. Pius X, July 1907

1962 A.D.: Before the Vatican Two Council began, Pope John XXIII, upon learning of the modernists' plan to attack the Canonized Latin Mass, issued his "binding" Apostolic Constitution, *Veterum Sapientia,* requiring the continued use of Latin as the language of the Latin Patriarchate, especially, as the language of the Mass. Despite Pope John's effort, Bishops, under "non-pope-ing popes" yielded to the evil, disobedient spirit of Vatican Two. In their refusal to implement Pope John's binding *Veterum Sapientia,* the Bishops (in the USA and throughout the world) seceded from the *semper ubique idem* Catholic Church, so as to constitute/form a "New Mass" and "new religion" (which, like the Anglican, kept up appearances, while being essentially at odds with Catholicism).

Veterum Sapientia

"Bishops and superiors-general of religious orders shall...ensure that in their seminaries where... [candidates] **are trained for the priesthood, all shall observe...the Apostolic See's decision...and obey these...prescriptions...they shall be on their guard...lest anyone under their jurisdiction...being eager for innovation...writes against the use of Latin in the ...higher sacred studies or in the liturgy... #15 ...We further commission the Sacred Congregation of Seminaries and Universities to prepare a syllabus for the teaching of Latin which all shall faithfully observe...Bishops in conference may indeed rearrange this syllabus...but they must never curtail it or alter its nature. Ordinaries may not ake it upon themselves to put their own proposals into effect....in virtue Our Apostolic Authority, We will and command that...this Our Constitution remain firmly established and ratified, notwithstanding anything to the contrary...."**

Pope John XXIII, *Veterum Sapientia,* (On Promoting the Study of Latin,Part II, Feb. 22, 1962 www.traditio.com/tradlib/latneces.txt

Who's To Blame For "New Mass?"

Let's make one thing clear. Vatican Two did not mandate or even conceive such a thing as "New Mass." However, the evil spirit of Vatican Two could be cited as a major contributing force. This "spirit of

Vatican Two told us what Vatican Two "meant to say" by its double-dutched nuances or even by what it did not say. Who defined these "esoteric imperatives?" Reigning experts did so, under duped Bishops and non-pope-ing Popes. Malachi Martin confirms that Vatican Two did not produce the Liturgical Revolt under which Catholics suffer:

> **"The Vatican Council said you must leave the priest's Latin Mass prayers the same ... The bishops voted this unanimously the last day of the council (in 1965) ...** [Instead] **Paul VI with Bugnini created a consilium** [a new council] **... to compose a new rite in contra-distinction to the Vatican Council.** [This is] **Paul VI's grave error!"**
> **Malachi Martin, Bernard Janzen audio tape, Triumph Comm.**

Was not Pope Paul VI the "head Bishop" of the Bishops' Liturgical Revolt? Also, while still a Bishop, Karol Wojtyla determined to destroy the Canonized Latin Mass. In light of his episcopal stand was Fr. Malachi Martin right in ascribing to him a noble intent to reform the self-destructing church?

> **"Certainly we will preserve the basic elements, the bread, the wine, but all else will be changed according to local traditions: words, gestures, color, vestments, chants, architecture, decor. The problem of liturgical reform is immense."**
> **Karol Wojtyla, Bishop of Krakow, *Mon Ami: Karol Wojtyla,* p. 220**

"Pope John Paul II [in the beginning of his reign in 1978] decided that in no way could he reform the church; he could not remove the [corrupt] bishops ... so he decided it's all over... nothing can save this organization ... it is thoroughly corrupt; Christ must be abandoning it ...'Christ has left you. The Mass is invalid,' [said the 'bacon priest,' who founded 'Church in Need'] ... He doesn't need you ... John Paul II saw that the source of grace was dried up ... The Roman Catholic Organization is a facade; it will implode; people are deserting it.

Malachi Martin, Bernard Janzen tapes, Triumph Communications

Certainly, both "Popes of the 'New Mass'" are guilty for not properly and plenarily pope-ing. Catholics can also blame the Bishops. Consider what Rev. Dr. Gommar De Pauw said:

"Today we have the exact carbon copy of the situation St. Pius X described in 1903, where he made it clear that the promoters of error today are not found among our declared enemies –the promoters of error today are found in the very ranks of our own Church! Today we are witnessing that exact situation.

We are also witnessing the very thing which was predicted in Fatima in 1917. And I could see right up, it's not exactly making that public. But I don't pretend to have the text of that message of Our Blessed Mother in Fatima, but the text I received in Rome has a few paragraphs there which are still very much of interest. It was predicted then and it is happening now.

"A time of severe trial is coming for the Church. Not today, nor tomorrow," the Blessed Mother said in 1917, but in the second half of the 20th century. Humanity will not develop as God desires it. Mankind will become sacrilegious and trample underfoot the gift it has received. No longer will order reign anywhere. "Even in the high places," the Blessed Mother predicted, "Satan will reign and direct the course of things. He will even succeed in infiltrating into the highest positions in the Church. Cardinals will oppose cardinals and bishops will oppose bishops. Satan will enter into their very midst. The Church will be obscured and all the world will be thrown into confusion."
Rev. Dr. Gommar de Pauw, *Conciliar or Catholic?* 1967, www.traditio,com

USA Bishops' Liturgical Revolution

On the feast of St. Peter's Chair, Pope John XXIII, in a most solemn ceremony, issued his *Veterum Sapientia,* which is related to us by Rev. Dr. Gommar de Pauw:

"In the full awareness of Our office and of Our authority, We decree and order ad Perpetuam Rei memoriam – in perpetuity," he [Pope John XXIII] **said. "We will and command that this Our constitution remain firmly established and ratified notwithstanding anything to the contrary..." And that constitution said**

that Latin had to stay in the liturgy and that the bishops had the obligation to see to it that no one under their authority works for the elimination of the Latin from either the liturgy or the studies for the priesthood in our seminaries. That was 8 months before the Vatican Council opened. And the Pope made it clear that this was ad Perpetuam Rei memoriam "for all perpetuity, this must remain in the fullness of Our authority We make this decision." he said...

And it was in that year, 1962, that a schismatic heretical, Conciliar sect of the Church in the United States of America was born. Why? Because regardless of the clear, solemn oath of Pope John XXIII, the majority of our American bishops refused to obey. I should know because I was there on the faculty at the time. And I had instructions from our Bishop in Baltimore NOT to implement the constitution from Rome. That's when I resigned.
Rev. Dr. Gommar de Pauw, *Conciliar or Catholic?* 1967 www.traditio.com

[After the Bishops' Liturgical Revolt began in earnest, Fr. de Pauw, who was Professor of Canon Law and Dean of Admissions at Mount St. Mary's Seminary in Emmitsburg, MD, resigned and founded the Catholic Traditionalist Movement, continuing to say Latin Mass in New York City. It was also through his efforts that the Latin Mass was broadcast by radio in many metropolitan areas of the U.S. He has kindly given permission to be quoted in this book.] Here is what Fr. de Pauw states in a lecture given in Chicago in 1967:

"I hesitated before I came here whether I should tell you this or not. ..But I decided, bad news as it is, I must give it to you. What you are attending today in the churches of our once Catholic Church establishment – what you are witnessing...is no longer a valid Sacrifice of the Mass.

That's a tremendous statement to make. So I have to prove it and I owe it to you to give the reasons...Here in...Chicago, between April 10 and 13 of this year (1967), our American bishops met in a luxury hotel and decided...that they would appeal to Rome...for permisssion to use an all-English Mass, including the Canon of the Mass...the most solemn part of the Canon, the Consecration.

Twenty-one bishops fought against it and voted against it. Out of more than 250...21 were still Catholic enough to warn their fellow bishops not to destroy the Latin Traditional Mass altogether –particularly, not to fool around with the *form* of Consecration, which affects the validity of the Mass....What I heard next was 'but once the majority of the American bishops decided to go for an all-English Mass, we who voted against it, decided not to break ranks and to go along with them.'...

What our American bishops proposed to Rome was an entirely new (English version) Canon of the Mass –a version which was totally heretical, a version in which three infallibly defined dogmas were eliminated. The dogma of the Divine Maternity of the Virgin Mary, defined in 431 by the Council of Ephesus–OUT. The

dogma of the Perpetual Virginity of the Virgin Mary, defined at the Lateran Council of 649–OUT. The dogma of the Divinity of Our Lord and Saviour Himself, defined at the Council of Nicaea in 325 – OUT....The word *blessed* has also been eliminated and so had the actual blessing...Ministers ...no longer bless the bread and wine...The answer...from Rome last September, was 'no." Twice... 'no.' *'We...cannot possibly permit you...to use this kind of Mass formula.'*

At one time...any Catholic bishop would have submitted immediately. No longer...Archbishop Deardon...president of the American Bishops Conference...in Rome for the Synod of Bishops... September 29...publicly announced that, even though Rome had rejected this English text of the Canon, we in the United States make it now mandatory in all public Masses and we will do it immediately, as soon as the printing can be done. ..If that isn't an open schism, then I don't know what a schism is....

What do we do now? ....
Rev. Dr. Gommar de Pauw, *Conciliar or Catholic?* 1967, www.traditio.com/tradlib/depauw67.txt

The True Church Believes and "Does" Only the Canonized Mass

"The just could exist more easily without the sun than without the Mass." **St. Leonard of Port Maurice**

In conclusion, we note that up until the Bishop's Revolt, (in the 1960's) there existed within the existential church complete and substantial "conformity to" every significant Christ-given and Church-canonized item of faith and morals (especially, liturgical morals). During these times, the Mass as Christ-given was not papally nor episcopally questioned nor challenged. It can plainly be seen that during the 1960's the "spirit of disobedience," the spirit of "anti-Christ" and "anti-Church," set in. This spirit informed and defined the Bishops' Liturgical Revolt, a revolt liturgically identified by its episcopal imposition of the "New Mass."

> **"When a foulness invades the whole Church...we must return to the Church of the past."**
>
> **St. Vincent of Lerins, *The Hidden Treasure***

One observes that Priests and Bishops who say the "New Mass" contradict, in word and deed, Church dogma concerning the Canonized Latin Mass Text. Thereby, they become gross heretics or apostates (according to St. Athanasius' definition of apostasy).

Chapter Three

"IN THE SPIRIT OF VATICAN TWO" BISHOPS REVOLT TO ESTABLISH "NEW MASS"

"Hence it must be clear to everyone that the controversy lately revived had already been definitely settled by the Apostolic See, and that it is to the insufficient knowledge of these documents that we must, perhaps, attribute the fact that any Catholic writer should have considered it still an open question." **Apostolicae Curae, Pope Leo XIII, 1896, No.22**

"New Mass Catholics" assure us that the church actually began at Vatican Two, even as "New Mass" writers and clerics will "quote the "pastoral" Council Vatican Two as if it were dogmatic when confronted with Christ-instituted, Church-defined dogma regarding the "law of prayer and the law of belief." "New Mass" propagandists incorrectly postulate that Trent (not Christ) invented the Canonized Mass. They assure us that, after Vatican Two, "alleged experts" were morally obliged to invent "the Mass of Vatican Two." This prevailing mindset rejects ever-binding authentic Catholic liturgical dogma in order to impose the revolutionary liturgical "big lie" which is "New Mass."

Post-Vatican Two existential or establishment clergy are largely opposed to the Catholic Church. The Bishops' "New Mass," has devolved into a "new religion," in which essential Catholic tenets have been changed or discarded. Only the facade and Catholic name have been retained. Obviously, the "new religion" of this existential church "bred in the 1960's" stands in opposition to the One, Holy, Catholic and Apostolic Church "of all time" founded by Jesus Christ. In truth, the Bishops use the ambiguous, veiled platform statements of Vatican Two (a non-dogmatic council) to establish and impose "New Mass" and its "new religion."

The episcopally defined and implemented disobedient spirit of Vatican Two affirmed and bestowed "divine rights on Bishops;" conferred a "common priesthood" on all; and thereby, redefined the identity and mission of the existential church. Bishops now blasphemously claim to be "living apostles, apostolic surrogates." They are so bold as to impose upon their clergy and laity a "New Mass" which liturgically embodies and evangelizes their own apostate religion–the rejection of the ever-binding "dogmatically Catholic" Council of Trent and the Christ-given and Church-canonized Latin Mass. "New Mass," by its own definition, is anti-Catholic.

> **Compared to the post-Tridentine epoch of the counter-reformation, Vatican Two represents in its fundamental characteristics, a 180 degree turn...It is a new church that has sprung up since Vatican Two.**
> **Hans Kung**

"New Mass" Bishops (including the Pope as Bishop of Rome) rejected Christ's Catholic Church. Unlike Protestant heretics of old who were outside the Church, these apostates within boldly claimed and enforced their "New Mass" as being the same Catholic Mass. "New Mass" (Novus Ordo Liturgy) replaced the Christ-instituted, Church-defined Canonized Latin Mass. However, "New Mass" clerics were not honest and did not rename their "new religion." Thereby, they claimed that the Catholic Church (especially, as defined by the Bishops' "New Mass") had so completely changed as to be "both the same, and yet, a whole new religion." The Rome-based Jesuit magazine *La Civilta Cattolica,* exclaimed victoriously:

> **With Vatican Council Two, the Tridentine age was brought to a close for the Church.**
> ***La Civilta Cattolica***

The existential church's new age, the anti-Tridentine age, enthrones "man" as the Bishops decide, the community celebrating the "New Mass. Thereby, "New Mass" liturgy outlaws and destroys an

essential characteristic and fruit of the Catholic liturgy–intimacy with the Divine:

> **"I am convinced that the crisis in the church that we are experiencing today is to a large extent due to the disintegration of the liturgy ... the community is celebrating only itself, an activity that is utterly fruitless."**
>
> ***Latin Mass,* Joseph Cardinal Ratzinger, June 2003**

Liturgy As "the People's Thing"

> **"We were assured that, as times change, so must ritual...we were told a million lies and half truths."**
>
> ***The Latin Mass,* Joseph Cardinal Ratzinger,Special Edition, 1966**

Joseph Cardinal Ratzinger confessed that liturgy has become "the people's thing." The Cardinal in charge of theology confessed the ugly truth. In spite of what blindly loyalist "New Mass" Catholics propagandize or "demonically believe," both Holy Ordered Priesthood and Holy Mass have been rejected. In turn, God's sentence sets in: "Ichabod!" Each community worships itself (as Bishops decide) but not God, as Christ decided. So has Cardinal Ratzinger verified and confirmed.

“New Mass” Enigmatic Definition of Liturgy

Liturgy is “the God-given way to praise God.” However, “New Mass” defines “liturgy” as “the work (ergos) of the people (laos).” Bugnini, the principal author of the “New Mass,” refined and applied this definition to focus on “celebration.” Liturgy of “New Mass” emphasizes the community “doing:” the “community realizes its holiness through celebration.”

> **“The** [new] **liturgy is theology in the form of prayer** [which rejects Christ’s priesthood]**. In its sensible signs...the whole public worship of the Mystical Body of Christ, *head and members,* is carried out.** p.39
>
> **All this begets a new attitude** [an anti-Catholic attitude] **... liturgical actions and sacramentals...should become a ‘celebration’...for the *salvation which Christ has*** [already once and forever over with] ***accomplished* and which the Church makes present** [as a mere prayerful recollection] **and operative for us in the Holy Spirit** [who is in us and who we are]. **Attention is *no longer focused on the minimum requirements for validity*** [since “New Mass” (Novus Ordo Liturgy) is invalid] **... but on the congregation that has gathered** [to celebrate “New Mass”]**...** p. 40
>
> **The liturgy is thus the unifying center of all the Church’s activity ... purpose** [of the liturgy] **... is to help**

human beings attain to full communion with God ... *salvation...which is made present in liturgical celebrations* [by the whole assembly] **the people...are to be led to a 'full, conscious and active participation in liturgical celebrations'...the celebration of the liturgy ... is the supreme manifestation of the Church...the liturgy is the *action of the people.*"**

The Reform of the Liturgy 1948-1975, p.39-42, brackets added

By deciphering Bugnini, the author of "New Mass," one comes to know the answer to the rhetorical intellectual puzzle: A tree that falls in the forest makes a noise only when a congregation gathers in "full, conscious and active participation in [liturgical] celebration [of its falling]." One no longer focuses on the "falling of the tree (validity)" but on the congregation that has gathered to celebrate its "long-time ago" falling. Welcome to "New Mass!" Welcome to the Bishops' "new religion!"

"New Mass" is Anti-Trent; Thereby Anti-Catholic

"We are now involved in a liturgy in which God is no longer the center of our attention...The human community has assembled for a commemorative meal. The assembly...is sitting there, face to face with the 'presider,' expecting from him, in accordance with the 'modern' spirit of the church, not so much a transfer of God's grace, but primarily some good ideas and advice on how to deal with daily life and its challenges."

Joseph Cardinal Ratzinger

Vatican Two, written in "double-dutch," is an excellent expression of the art of "double-talk." In spite of its evil bias, Vatican Two can be "rewritten and expressed" in Catholic terms (much as a student's bad paper could be rewritten into a good paper). *De facto,* the Holy Spirit of the Catholic Church and, especially, the Holy Spirit of Trent was rejected and the "disobedient spirit of Vatican Two" is the tool used to interpret and implement what is alleged to be Vatican Two. Indeed, here is the heart of "New Mass."

The Council of Trent is dogmatic. In contrast, Vatican Two is not dogmatic *(in se)* and the (reigning) spirit of Vatican Two is heretical, especially, as being anti-Christ. The Catholic Church, as specified by the dogmatic Council of Trent defined the Priest as Christ-priest; the one who celebrates the Mass and sacraments. The Christ-priest (*ex officio, in persona Christi)* provides or brings about proper worship, sacrificing at the altar and forgiving sins sacramentally. Within each Catholic parish, the "person in charge" of the salvation of souls, and, the praise of God is the Holy Ordered Priest, whereas, "New Mass" abides with a mere facilitator or presider in its faith community.

The Church of the Counter-Reformation, triumphing over Protestant negations, presented itself as "the

Church of the New and Eternal Christ-Covenant, the Church of Holy Sacrifice and Holy Sacrament." Christ, not man, was the focal point of liturgy. "New Mass" liturgy is the work of man. It is celebrated by man for man. In "New Mass," alleged "priests" are "co-ministers with the laity both of the liturgy and of the Good News," sent into the world, involved in it, for a more authentic service of man.

It is stupefying and scandalous that nearly the entire Catholic Bishopric adopted, without resistance, this fundamental premise of a universal fraternity, a veritable contradiction of Divine Revelation and the foundation of an anti-Christ humanism. This fundamental creed is Masonic, not Christian. God is said to be the Father of all. Consequently, all are brothers and sisters. Any and all discrimination must be abolished. The "New Mass" embodies and evangelizes such New Age or apocalyptic apostasy.

"New Mass" Destroys the Holy Ordered Priesthood

"There are few people left who speak of the Holy Mass as the Sacrifice of the New Covenant...offered to God the Father through Jesus Christ, or of the sacramental

union with Christ that we experience when we receive Holy Communion. Today, we are dealing with 'holy bread' to be shared among us as a sign of our brotherhood with Jesus."

Joseph Cardinal Ratzinger

In "New Mass," the satanic spirit embraced by the Bishops destroyed the Holy Sacrifice and the "here and now source" of this Holy Sacrifice–the Canonized (by Christ Himself and then by His Church) Holy Ordered Priesthood, whereby men are metamorphosized into Christ-priests. How was the rejection of Holy Orders brought about by Vatican Two? The Bishops' "New Mass" requires a "new ministry," which did not offer sacrifice and sacrament. Thus, the Bishops redefined their priests instituting their own "New Ordinal," elevating the laity to ministry; and like the Anglican Bishops before them, rendered obsolete and, therefore, "null and void as Holy Ordered Priests" their ill-begotten ministers. Again, one perceives the poisonous fountainhead of evil in the New Order: "New Mass" begat "new religion" begat "new ministers" begat "New Ordinal." Did not the Bishops repeat the Anglican schism?

At the Council, Bishops claimed divine apostolic rights and attempted something they could not do: in effect, they bestowed their "New Mass" version of

"priesthood" on the laity, which included exorbitantly ascribing responsibilities to them in virtue of their "common priesthood."

What were the sovereign Bishops to do with priests (who can be likened to " episcopal fetuses," most of which fail to develop to their full potential and be born as "Bishops")? Being stuck with them, they were clumsily fit into Newchurch. The *Decree on Priestly Training* let this be understood:

> **Animated by the spirit of Christ, this sacred synod is fully aware that the desired renewal of the whole church depends to a great extent on the ministry of its priest...**
>
> ***Decree on Priestly Training***

Episcopally commissioned presiders or facilitators (a.k.a. "priests") facilitate laymen to fulfil their own priestly roles, especially, to celebrate "New Mass." Priests are to "collaborate" with Bishops; and, under their strict supervision, preside over the exercise of the common priesthood they share with the laity. As their commissioning rite now makes clear: they are "ordained" *to receive the gifts of the people of God. No longer are they "ordained". to offer the Holy Sacrifice of the Mass.*

The "New Ordinal" brings out the fact that Holy

Ordered priests are now replaced by men commissioned as episcopal collaborators and "New Mass" (Novus Ordo Service) presiders or facilitators. Here is Satan's greatest and dual ecclesial victory: in "New Mass," Christ's Mass and Holy Ordered Christ-priests have been destroyed. Seven years after the Council, the Abbe de Nantes diagnostic was impressive:

> **When good priests, in obedience to their bishops, will have sufficiently distanced themselves from what is divine and lost themselves in what is human, they will come to realize that they have been 'had'... it will be too late ... The Priesthood was great, solid and prosperous, as long as it defined itself by its intimate relation to God in worship and in the apostolate which relates to it. And I add: priests were happy. However, Priesthood has deteriorated; and beginning with the day that it turned towards men, so as to occupy priests with the things of the earth and no longer with those of Heaven, it has been destroyed. This is the episcopal crime committed against the Priesthood.**
>
> **Abbe de Nantes, *CCR*, n 25, p. 9**

"Although it clearly follows...that the Pope can err at times and command things which should not be done, that we are not to be simply obedient to him in all things.... To know in what cases he is to be obeyed...it is said in the Acts of the Apostles: 'One ought to obey God rather than man;' therefore, were the Pope to command anything against ... the truth of the Sacraments... he ought not to be obeyed...."
Summa de Ecclesia, 1489, based on doctrine formulated and defined by the Council of Florence and Pope Eugenius IV and Pope Pius IV

"Peter is subject to the duties of the Office; otherwise, neither is the Church in him, nor is he in the Church."
St. Thomas Aquinas, *Summa Theologica,* IIa IIae, Q.39, Art. 1, ad 6

"It is beyond question that the Pope can error even in matters touching the faith...Many pontiffs were heretics. The last of them was Pope John XXII (1316-1334)."
Pope Adrian VI (1522-1523) Quaest. In IV Sent.; quoted in Viollet, *Papal Infallibility and the Syllabus,* 1908

Chapter Four

THE QUESTION OF VALIDITY

"Novelty is a sure mark of heresy."
St. Vincent of Lerins

Definition of Valid / Invalid

valid–that which is necessary to produce the desired [Christ-given or Christ-intended] effect: that action of a priest which is spiritually effective.

licit–that which is permited by law, whether civil or ecclesial. Often distinguished from valid, to express what the law prescribes or allows, as distinct from what is necessary to produce the desired effect. Lawful, allowed, permitted.
***Pocket Catholic Dictionary,* John A. Hardon, S.J., Image Books, New York, 1980**

Since Fr. Hardon's definition of validity is based on Pope Leo XIII's dogmatic *Apostolicae Curae,* it is adopted as our own. *Apostolicae Curae* leads one to realize that validity is determined by all of the religiously meaningful words used in any "service," which is presented as a Mass, as well as, by the "very nature of the service;" (e.g. The Anglican and the

Bishops' "New Mass" reject the dogmatic Council of Trent's definition of the Mass; and "New Mass" restructures liturgy to celebrate "man"). The religion "of, in or from" the Anglican "Mass-Liturgies;" or, in *Apostolicae Curae's* terms, "the native character and spirit" of this liturgy prove the Anglican Liturgy to be invalid – to be salutarily null and void.

This "invalidating reasoning," which applies to the Anglican "New Mass" renders it dogmatically invalid. This same Leonine reasoning, which led to the Anglican "New Mass" being dogmatically pronounced invalid, applies "even more so," to the Bishops' "New Mass."

Therefore, one can see why Fr. Hardon's definiton is so useful. He has taken into account the big picture. Form [known by or perceived from the words added to, omitted from or modified relative to the Canonized Latin Mass Text (from *"Suscipe Sancte Pater...*through *Per Ipsum..."*)]determines the "native character and spirit" of any alleged Mass-Liturgy.

Most traditionalists do not share Pope Leo's definition; at least, wholeheartedly and with full consent. They tend to narrow-mindedly define a

"Mass" as valid if it contains the eight "magic" words – "This is my body" and "This is my blood." They don't want to face the unavoidable conclusion (in the light of *Apostolicae Curae)* that an invalid "New Mass" has been illicitly, episcopally imposed upon the faithful to the effect of producing a "new religion" which is at odds with Christ's Catholic Church. Today, for the first time in church history, the existential church is in a state of "apostasy within,"the product of the Bishops' Revolt of the 1960's.

Mad Hatter Notions of Validity

> **"Modernist heretics hold that the formulas which we call dogma must be subject to vicissitudes and are, therefore, liable to change. Thus the way is open to the intrinsic evolution of dogma. Here we have an immense structure of sophisms which ruin and wreck all religion."** ***Pascendi Dominici Gregis,*** **Pope St. Pius X, 1907**

The Canonized Latin Mass was instituted by Christ; comes to us through and from Apostolic Tradition; and, word-for-word, was dogmatically canonized in perpetuity by the *sensus et praxis fidelium,* and "officially so" by Christ's Church. This is

undeniable Catholic fact. This is Catholic dogma. The Canonized Latin Mass Text (especially, the Offertory and Consecration) is not the plaything of the existential church. It is God's most Sacred Gift from Apostolic Times.

The Christ-instituted and Church-dogmatized Canonized Latin Mass Text comes to us as a perfect diamond. Any change of this diamond destroys it. More than anything else, it is to be "applied" and handed down intact. Such is the essential duty of the priestly class, especially, of the "Pope as Priest." The prophetic class is to insure that the priests perform their most important duty – to "apply and hand on intact" the Canonized Mass Text (to the next generation of priests). The "Pope as Prophet and King" is primarily obligated to do so.

A significant or substantial change in the religion of the Mass as dogmatized by Trent has materialized in the "New Mass." Mad Hatters (those allegedly dedicated to the traditional Mass) as it were, readily grant "New Mass" the right to alter the most precious and perfect diamond. However, they demand it be altered as they decide. They fail to realize that any significant "addition to" or "subtraction from;" or, modification of the core prayers of the Canonized Form of the Canonized

Latin Mass Text, *ipso facto,* renders the subsequent bastardized version of the Canonized Latin Mass invalid (spiritually ineffective). It is obvious that many in the Latin Mass movement who maintain an allegiance to "New Mass" basic theology, do not believe in the Canonized Latin Mass Text (as having been instituted by Christ) and, therefore, as necessary for all Catholics to believe (under penalty of apostasy). If one were truly dedicated to Christ's Mass; and if one accepted the dogmatically established and applied principles of *Apostolicae Curae* to establish validity, one would reject any and all mind-sets which tolerate, presume or advocate "liturgical evolution" or "a reform of the liturgical reform" or "living with religious diversity within the Church.

The Papal Problem

> **"If anyone says that the received and approved rites of the Catholic Church, accustomed to be used in the administration of the Sacraments, may be despised or omitted by the ministers without sin and at their pleasure, or may be changed by any pastor (a term that includes the Supreme Pastor, the Pope) of the churches to other new ones, let him be anathema."**
>
> **19th Dogmatic Ecumenical Council, Trent, 1545-1563**

"It's a whole new church since Vatican II; and I like it!" --Vatican II "Catholic"

In a vain attempt to justify their acceptance of the "New Mass," some Mad Hatters believe that whatever a reigning pope apparently allows and approves in a non-dogmatic way, must be considered as "binding Catholic truth." In effect, they perceive papal non-dogmatic contemporary "New Mass" liturgical allowances to be so binding as to "make null and void" any or all preceding dogmatic binding papal decrees. Therefore, according to this particular way of thinking, if one were to see the horrible truth that the "New Mass" Liturgy is *in se* (or, in itself) conclusively invalid, one must continue to profess the contrary to remain a Catholic. Welcome to the world of Alice in Liturgical Wonderland!

A few "Mad Hatters agree with "New Mass" and make the reigning papal "who" infallible, in opposition to the Catholic set of "dogmas" or "whats" required to be held in order to be a Catholic. Even here, they arbitrarily rule out the infallibility of any past "not-presently-reigning" papal "who" such as Pope St. Pius V. Others, who see that "New Mass" is not valid, stay sane (still contending that the pope cannot allow an invalid Mass Liturgy) by postulating that he is not really the pope – but rather, that the "seat is empty" (sedis vacantis). Both camps are

wrong, but, at least, sede vacantists avoid becoming irrational "liturgical psychotics."

However, is there another possible solution? Could popes and prelates be so evil as to allow and promote "the abominable desolation"– the unholy in place of the Most Holy? Since we witness that they do so before our very eyes, one must conclude that they can do so. What is, is possible; and, what is, has also been predicted and verified by "authorities." (Additionally, none of us has the urgency nor the official capacity to dogmatically pronounce a pope not to be a pope. Therefore, one should avoid "dogmatizing sedis vacantism.")

> **"In drafting the definition of the Dogma of Infallibility in 1869, the periti of Vatican Council I actually discovered that more than forty popes had preached personal doctrinal errors in preceding centuries, though not in an infallible context."**
> **www.traditio.com, The Limitations of Papal Authority, p.11**

Properly Defining "Validity"

> **"In the Catholic Church Herself every care must be taken that we may hold fast to that which has been believed everywhere, always and by all. For this is truly and properly Catholic."** **St. Vincent Lerins, 450 A.D.**

The Church rejects the notion that validity can be established by the existence of the words of consecration, especially, the existence of eight "magic" words ("This is My Body; this is My Blood.") The proof of this is rather simple and straightforward. The Anglican Service has many of the established words of consecration (and all of the "eight magic words") – far more than "New Mass." Yet the Anglican Service is dogmatically defined to be invalid or null and void; spiritually ineffective in producing the Holy Sacrifice of the Mass as instituted by Christ.

Within the context of total conformity to the dogma of Christ's Canonzied Latin Mass Liturgy, in the gravest of emergencies, one can employ *"Hoc est... and Hic est..."* to confirm the "Holy Ordered confection" of a valid Mass. However, considering the validity of any anti-dogmatic or anti-canonical Mass-simulation demands an entirely different approach, taking into account the dogmatic decision of *Apostolicae Curae* – that Anglican Services are invalid or "null and void" because they have a native character and spirit (a religion) antithetical to "producing a valid Mass."

Chapter Five

THE "NEW MASS" IN GENERAL

"The Holy Ghost was not promised to the successor of Peter for them to make a new doctrine known, but for them to maintain in a holy way, the revelation transmitted by the Apostles, that is, the Deposit of Faith."
The Dogmatic Vatican One Council

"With malice aforethought, lying propagandists in liberal disguise" deviously postulate that Trent invented "the Tridentine Mass." In this manner, they vainly attempt to justify their institution of what they label as the "Mass of Vatican Two." This modernist mind-set rejects authentic Catholic liturgical dogma in order to impose the diabolic liturgical "big lie" that "Mass" evolved and will always evolve.

There exists no sound basis for denying the basic liturgical dogma of the Church concerning the origin and "make up" of "the Canonized Latin Mass." Christ Himself instituted the Canonized Latin Mass. This is Church-dogmatized truth. In agreement with the spirit and letter of the binding, dogmatic Council of Trent, one is led to conclude that only demonic

pride could account for any priest's consciously and willingly abandoning the Canonized Latin Mass Text designed by Christ in order to embrace a sacrilegious man-made text.

> **"Holy things must be treated in a holy way and this Sacrifice is the most holy of all things. And so, that this Sacrifice might be worthily and reverently offered and received, the Catholic Church many centuries ago specified** [permanently established or dogmatized, because authored by Christ] **this Sacred Canon. It is free from all error** (See D.B. 953) **and contains nothing that does not savor strongly of holiness and piety and nothing that does not raise to God the minds of those who offer the Sacrifice."**
>
> **D.B. 942, ch.4, Canon of the Mass, Council of Trent**

This dogmatic Council (Trent) decreed the moral impossibility of any dogmatic change. Pope Paul VI acknowledged this dogma when he referred to his "New Mass" as a "novelty," admitting that, in exchanging the Mass for "a novelty," we were "giving up something of priceless worth."

According to Pope Paul VI, "New Mass" is the "people's conversing with God." Such a "New Mass" (text) cannot be validly utilized (i.e. to bring about the most precious Salutary Reality-- Christ's Saving Will--realized on earth as it is in Heaven):

> **The new rites of Mass ... affect our hereditary patrimony ... We are giving up something of priceless worth ... this novelty ... is no small thing ...** [We now implement a service] **... which shows that the faithful are qualified to have a supernatural conversation with God.** (brackets added)
>
> ***L'Osservatore Romano,*** **Pope Paul VI, Nov. 28, 1969**

Why did Pope Paul VI refer to the many variations of "New Mass" as a *novelty?* Was he flaunting an infallible, dogmatic Church Council? Was he making an implicit confession that he really was not a valid Pope? Was he tricked or *"skillfully led to believe"* [Bugnini's words: *The Reform of the Liturgy:1948-1975*] that he, as Pope, could virtuously replace the Canonized Latin Mass with a "novelty?" Was he blind-sided by his so-called "experts?" Regardless, he "green-lighted" mega-sacrilegious, heretical novelty-- the wholesale episcopal imposition of this alien rite liturgy in the place of Christ's Holy Canonized Mass Liturgy for the Latin Rite.

> **Those, therefore, who, after the manner of wicked heretics, dare to set aside ecclesiastical traditions, and to invent any kind of novelty, or to reject any of those things entrusted to the Church, or who wrongfully and outrageously devise the destruction of any of those traditions enshrined in the Catholic Church, are to be punished thus: if they are bishops, we order them to be deposed; but, if they are monks or laymen, we command them to be excluded from the community.**
>
> **Second Council of Nicea, 787 A.D.**

Again, consider the "papal problem." If one assumes or believes that "the Pope cannot merely permit the "New Mass" but that he must be canonizing or validating such by his permitting it," then one must either conclude that the "New Mass" is not what it obviously or conclusively is: invalid; or, that the Pope is not the Pope. The choice is clear.

Such an unwarranted and anti-Catholic theory of papal power has produced strange fellow travelers. As people like Michael Davies, as it were, look to their sides, they find the sede-vacantists. These "vacant seaters" assume what Michael Davies assumes: that "the 'Pope' cannot permit evil on a wholesale level without dogmatizing the evil." However, they seem to be "more logical." ***Sedis vacantists cannot believe that evil becomes good or that evil becomes dogma by its being papally tolerated or supported.*** **Instead, they choose the "more logical" alternative: "the 'New Mass' is, indeed, conclusively invalid;" and, therefore, sedis vacantists stipulate that "these Popes who allow it are not really Popes."**

A similar period of confusion occurred in the time of St. Jerome. He observed that ninety percent of the Bishops were Arians. No small matter that they denied the divinity of Christ. Now, nearly all Bishops

deny Christ and His Mass to embrace an "anti-Mass." No small matter that Bishops now "discard, in order to sacrilege (with a Mass-simulation)" the Christ-given, Church dogmatized, "formula" to bring about the mystical/ sacramental presence of the Sacred Heart, the living essence of Catholicism.

Faith and Morals, Not Prelates "Whats" Not "Whos"

> **For the doctrine of faith as revealed by God has not been presented to men as a philosophical system to be perfected by his own ingenuity; it was presented as a divine trust...to be faithfully kept and infallibly interpreted. It also follows that any meaning of the sacred dogmas that has once been declared by Holy Mother Church, must always be retained; and there must never be any deviation from that meaning on the specious grounds of a more profound understanding** (see 83, can.3). **'Therefore, let there be growth...and all possible progress in understanding, knowledge, and wisdom in each man...as well as, in the entire Church, according to the stage of their development; but only within proper limits, that is, in the same doctrine, in the same meaning, and in the same purport.'**
>
> **First Vatican Council, ch 4, DS no. 80**

Through His Apostles, Christ bequeathed to His

Church a set of faith and morals. The essential Catholic Church is defined by the "whats" of the Deposit of Faith (which closed at the death of the last Apostle). The "whos" of the existential church are obliged to hold, preserve, "apply intact," and faithfully hand on the "whats" of Catholicism. Otherwise, "in reality," (whether Popes, Bishops, or even theologians) they are cut off from the Catholic Church (Christ's Mystical Body).

Ultimately, the only "Who" one believes in and adores is God. Ecclesial infallibility concerns "whats," and not "who." Technically speaking, *in se*, no prelate, not even a pope is personally infallible. In effect, papal infallibility means papally "graced capability and responsibility" for assuring universal belief in or "conformity to" each and every One, Holy, Catholic, Apostolic (already decreed) 'what.'"

The "whats" popes have *"de fide* pronounced," for example, the Canonized Latin Mass (for the Latin Rite) were, since Apostolic times, are now and will always be dogmatically, infallibly true; binding on all Catholics, past, present and to come. These "whats," like unto Christ, are the same yesterday, today and forever. Being "in and from" Apostolic Tradition, they bind forever. To purposely deny any of them (e.g. that only the Canonized Latin Mass is

the Mass of the Latin Rite) is to become a heretic and, thereby, an apostate. To practice such in liturgy is to be in a state of liturgical apostasy (within the anti-Catholic ecclesial establishment).

Belief in the Catholic Church is belief in the "whats" or the "contents within" Apostolic Tradition or the Deposit of Faith. A very few of these "whats" have been papally "high-lighted" (as being relevant to correct or to condemn contemporary apostasies within the Latin Patriarchate) by being *"de fide* canonized" by popes. These *"de fide"* dogmas (such as Christ's Canonized Latin Mass Liturgy or *extra ecclesiam nulla salus*) are doubtlessly and gravely binding.

Be aware that to do the opposite of the *de fide dogma* (e.g. as a Holy Ordered priest or as a "fake priest," to say any "New Mass") is an act of apostasy. Likewise, laymen knowingly participating in "New Mass" are apostatizing.

Catholic belief in the Catholic Church is not belief in any human person. Pope idolatry is a gross sin, not virtue. "The head of the Church is Jesus Christ. The Pope is...the visible vicar of Christ...he is bound on all sides by the constitution of the Church, as...given...by Christ" (*The Early Papacy to the Synod of Chalcedon in 451,* pp.27-28).

Nota Bene

"St. Cajetan points out that the famous axiom *'Ubi Petrus, ibi Ecclesia' [Where the Pope is, there is also the Church]* holds true only when the Pope acts and behaves as the Pope, because Peter 'is subject to the duties of the Office;' otherwise, 'neither is the Church in him, nor is he in the Church.'"
Apud St. Thomas Aquinas, *Summa Theologica,* IIa IIae, Q.39, Art.1, ad 6

Repeating Catholic dogma, note well that, whenever any Pope (after St. Peter) attains his office, the fact is that the Catholic Church has already been infallibly or immutably defined. In fact, the essence of Catholicism is to be found in all of the "whats" which define one's open-ended and unqualified allegiance to the one "Who." All of these "whats" are immutably contained within "Apostolic Tradition"–which was closed at the death of the last Apostle. No one, not even an angel from Heaven, can add to, modify or subtract from, this Deposit of Faith. Even if what appears to be an angel does so, one must curse such a creature to eternal Hell (Gal 1:8). *A fortiori,* regarding "less Heavenly beings," one must never follow any prelate who dares to oppose any "Catholic Apostolic 'what:'"

> **"Such is the value of Tradition that even Encyclicals and other documents of the ordinary teaching of the Sovereign Pontiff are only infallible in those teachings that are confirmed by Tradition, or under various**

> **Popes and over a long period. If, therefore, an act of the ordinary magisterium of a Pope disagrees with the teaching guaranteed by the magisterial tradition of several Popes and for a considerable time, it should not be accepted. Therefore, in full harmony with the Church, all priests may continue to celebrate the traditional Mass of St. Pius V."**
>
> Bishop Antonio deCastro Mayer, Brazil, Pastoral Letter, 1971

The ecclesiastical hierarchy was instituted by God to faithfully transmit the Deposit of the Faith, especially, its "Living Sacred Heart." Christ appointed a Vicar to whom He gave the authority and grace to accomplish this awesome sacred task. His authority is limited to "upholding the 'whats' contained within the Deposit of Faith–those 'whats' which always have the same meaning and the same sense" (Denzinger 1800)**. Vatican I clearly taught that:**

> **"The Holy Spirit has not been promised to Peter's successors in order that they might reveal, under His inspiration, new doctrine, but in order that, with His help, they may carefully guard and faithfully expound the revelation as it was handed down by the Apostles, that is to say, the Deposit of Faith."**
>
> ***Pastor Aeternus Pastor* Denziger, 1836**

Hence, it follows that papal authority applies only to "matters" which fall within the parameters of the Deposit of Faith. For example, to replace the Mass "of and from Apostolic Tradition" would be an evil

deed which must be rejected. To be binding, any papal exercise of authority must fall clearly and entirely within the bounds of orthodoxy; and this is true concerning the Liturgy. The Pope may indeed abrogate any of the decisions of his predecessors, but always and only within the limits of orthodoxy. As the *Catholic Encyclopedia* states:

> **"The scope of this infallibility is to preserve the Deposit of Faith revealed to man by Christ and His Apostles."**
> *The Catholic Encyclopedia,* 1908

Therefore, any papally edicted legislation (or "what") which abrogates dogma, or attempts to change the meaning of the constant teaching of the Church, would step outside the bounds of orthodoxy. The Canonized Latin Mass for the Latin Rite, having been instituted by Christ, dogmatized by His Church, and having been the constant teaching of the Church since its inception, clearly falls beyond and outside the jurisdiction of any power of papal abrogation. Despite the fact that the Roman Congregation refused permission for the Bishops' "New Mass," Popes Paul VI and John Paul II, in their refusal to "properly pope," ambiguously "imply permission or toleration" of "New Mass."

“New Mass” Renders Existential Church Apostate

“One must resist to his face a Pope who publicly destroys the Church.”
– *De Comparata Auctoritate Papae et Concilio,* cap. XXVII apud Victoria

“New Mass” is not the Mass of the Catholic Church. It is the Mass-simulating liturgical service which constitutes or defines an alien “new religion.” It is grossly “contrary to” or “in contradiction with” the Catholic Church as One, Holy, Catholic and Apostolic; and, thereby, it renders itself apostate.

♦ **Christ’s Church is One.** From Pentecost until the end of the world, Christ’s Church is One: *semper, ubique idem* (always and everywhere the same). It is one or the same in space and time; in space, all over the world; in time, in each time, the same as in all other times. “New Mass” is certainly not “one” with the Church Liturgy in and from Apostolic Tradition. Both Anglican and the Bishops’ “New Masses” embody a bold and major rejection of Christ’s Catholic Church being “One” and Apostolic, (as well as, Holy and Catholic). They are apostate, sacrilegious liturgies. In the words of Pope Leo XIII, they are “null and void!”

♦ **Christ’s Church is Apostolic–once, for all times defined by the Apostles** (in the New Testament and/or the "Deposit of Faith"). Divine Revelation ceased at the death of the last Apostle.[For Catholics, the Deposit of Faith (credenda one must believe to be saved) is from Christ and is to be found in Apostolic Tradition.] The Deposit of Faith (the collection of Catholic credenda) was closed forever at the death of the last Apostle. Any and all "New Mass" liturgies, not being "One;" and, not being "Apostolic," are apostate or *extra ecclesiam;* and, as such, damn souls to Hell. *In se,* these "fake Masses" cannot save souls. *Extra ecclesiam nulla salus.*

♦ **Christ's Church is Holy.** It is holy,as Christ defined it to be holy: as containing the Most Holy Sacrifice and Sacrament (*as instituted by Christ* and as irreformably canonized by His Church). Without the Mass as instituted by Christ and canonized by His Church, no church body can claim to be holy, (the Source or Locus of the Holy Spirit's salutary actions, in this age of the Holy Spirit). "New Mass" exists without the Most Holy Sacrifice and Sacrament.The Bishops have excised the living mystical/sacramental Holy Sacrifice and Holy Sacrament of Christ from the Latin Patriarchate. "Ichabod!" The salutary Sacred Heart has been rejected by the wicked, revolting Bishops.

♦ **Christ's Church is "Catholic."** *De facto,* (as was apparent until the Bishops' Liturgical Revolt) a church was considered Catholic only if it provided the Mass, the Most Holy, Christ-given and Church-defining Gift of

God. Christ gave His Body and Blood (Holy Sacrifice and Holy Sacrament) as the New and Eternal Testament to His Church to be continuous, unto the end of time; according to the specific instructions He gave to His Apostles (Eastern and Latin Rite). The Catholic Church from Apostolic times, in practice and in belief, *(secundum praxem et fidem)* irreformably canonized certain Mass formulae.

From Apostolic Times until the end of time, only that existential church which uses a Christ-instituted and Church-canonized Mass Liturgy can claim to be Catholic. Even today, for the ordinary Catholic, after confirming one's Catholicism, the usual question then asked is: "Where do you go to Mass?" Indeed, one cannot be a follower of Christ without "having the Mass" (as defined by the Catholic Church).

~~~~~~

"...The Pope could be schismatic, if he were unwilling to be in normal union with the whole body of the Church...or...if he wished to overturn the rites of the Church based on Apostolic Tradition."

Francisco Suarez, S.J. (1548-1617) called by Pope Paul V *"Doctor Eximius–Most Exalted and Pious;"* considered the greatest theologian of the Society of Jesus.

The Limitations of Papal Authority, p. 8

See www.traditio.com.

~~~~~~

WORDS OF POPE PAUL VI vs. WORDS OF POPE ST. PIUS X

Pope Paul VI:
"...How can such a change be made? ... Answer: ...It is a law...thought out by authoritative experts of Sacred Liturgy... What exactly are the changes? ... Answer: "...Many new directions for celebrating the rites...nothing has been changed... of our traditional Mass...Some may...think...diminution of truths...are sanctioned by it...that the law of prayer, *lex orandi* and the law of faith, *lex credendi,* is compromised...Absolutely not...The Mass of the new rite is and remains the same Mass we have always had...its sameness has been brought out more clearly...What will be the results of this innovation?...the faithful will participate...do not talk about 'the new Mass,'....Let us...speak of the 'new epoch' in the Church..." **Pope Paul VI, General Audience, 11/19/1969**

"...Turn your minds...to the liturgical innovation of the new Mass...[it] affects our hereditary religious patrimony...ceremonies at the altar...no longer...carried out with the same words and gestures...prepare for this many-sided incovenience...caused by every novelty...pious persons are disturbed most...priests may feel some annoyance...we should find out...about this innovation...take into account the motives for this grave change...the first is obedience to the council...obedience now implies obedience to the Bishops... the faithful are...invested with... 'royal priesthood'...qualified to have a supernatural conversation with God...greatest newness [is] the newness of language...no longer Latin...parting with the speech of...centuries...we are becoming like profane intruders in the literary preserve of sacred utterance... We have reason for regret...for bewilderment...we are giving up something of priceless worth...but a profound participation by every single one present, and an outpouring of spirit in community charity...will help to make the Mass...a school of ...peaceful but demanding Christian sociology...."

Pope Paul VI, General Audience, 11/26/1969

POPE ST. PIUS X:
"One of the primary obligations assigned by Christ to the office committed to Us of feeding the Lord's flock is that of guarding with the greatest vigilance the Deposit of Faith delivered to the Saints, rejecting the profane novelties of words, and the gainsaying of knowledge falsely so-called...We may no longer keep silent [against the modernists] lest we should seem to fail in our essential duty."

Pope St. Pius X, *Pascendi Dominici Gregis,*, 9/8/1907

Man's Mass Not Christ's Mass

"It is not my intention to prohibit the Tridentine Mass."
Pope Paul VI to Cardinal Heenan, 11/19/69

The Canon (defined as the priest's prayers from *"Suscipe sancte Pater....*through *Per Ipsum... ")* is the principal and essential part of the Canonized Texts of Christ's Canonized Latin Mass. Because it derives from Christ, it is protected by the Church's most binding laws. The Bishops' "New Mass" service is not instituted by Christ; the Bishops' "New Mass" is not canonized by His Church.

"Worship used to be addressed to God as an homage. Henceforth, it will be addressed to man to console and enlighten him."
Fr. Martin Luther

As with the Sacraments, Christ instituted the Mass. Bugnini instituted "New Mass." Bugnini and his accomplices confessed that their purpose was to make the Catholic ritual "not Catholic." Indeed, they succeeded. Once again, as happened in the Protestant Revolt, man becomes the *raison d'etre* of the new "bogus Christian" Services.

"In the 'New Mass,' men gather together to celebrate their presumption-based communal 'Christ-ed-ness.'"
Fr. Paul Trinchard

From "Leo XIII / Fatima" onward, the devil has imposed his New Age Spirit upon the cooperative or duped majority: man has been enthroned; God has been dethroned. The Bishops' "New Mass" ritualizes this demonic disobedient spirit and happening. Thus, it "sacrileges" the Christ-instituted Mass.

> **"The devil has succeeded in infiltrating evil under the appearance of good...worst of all, the devil has succeeded in leading into error and deceiving souls having a heavy responsibility through the positions they hold."**
>
> **Sister Lucia of Fatima**

The philosophical/societal groundwork for the Bishops' Liturgical Apostasy (as the enthronement of man and the dethronement of God) was initially conceived in the time of Pope Leo XIII and the Fatima Revelation. Both the Pope and the Fatima Revelation addressed this conception. Pope Leo himself had a vision wherein the devil would be given one hundred years or so of greater freedom to destroy Christ's one and only Church on earth. One could contend that the "devil's century" began with the "latest year" in which the Third Secret (which is still not revealed) was to be told–1960, the beginning of Vatican Two. Inspired by God, Pope Leo XIII predicted the abomination of impiety, "New Mass.". Read the original Leonine Prayer as it explicitly predicts that *"Abominable impiety would issue from the papal throne."* The "New Mass" liturgy is abominable impiety! The "New Mass" issued from Pope Paul VI as Bishop of Rome, "as from the papal throne."

Fatima prepares us; fortifies us against; and predicts these apocalyptic times. Fatima begins with angels adoring and giving the Holy Sacrament (which is born from Christ's Holy Sacrifice of Mass) to the children. It is interesting to note the Catholic "universality" of Fatima–the Holy Sacrament was given to Jacinta and Francisco under the "species of wine," (following the Apostolic origination of the "Eastern custom").

Fatima climaxed before thousands of witnesses (October 13, 1917). In this public vision of the Miracle of the Sun, the sun represents the existential church. It gave out or tolerated many hues or colors. It failed to be the sun! Furthermore, the sun (the existential church) threatened to destroy all of the people as it fell from the sky. A slightly different version demonstrating the identity of the Church with Christ's Mass is reflected by St. Leonard of Port Maurice: the sun = Christ's Mass, which has fallen from its "one and only" place in the Church:

> **"The just could exist more easily without the sun than without the Mass. Does not God spare each justified sinner for the sake of the One Just One and His continuing Sacrifice of the Mass?"**
>
> *The Hidden Treasure,* St. Leonard of Port Maurice

Within the Latin Rite, all modern Marian apparitions, from Guadalupe onward, focused on the Mass. One of the greatest salutary theophanies of all times was given to Sister Lucy at Tuy, Spain: the vision of the Canonized Mass. Mass is salvation by the Blessed Trinity through Christ's Holy Sacrifice. Graces from Christ's Holy Sacrifice, by God's freely chosen dispensation, come through Our Lady. The Mass is the Source of all grace and mercy to us "naturally Hell-bound sinners;" and yet, by cooperation with God's graces, we can become supernaturally repentant sinners. However, the Mass, as the Source of grace for sinners, is now missing within existential Catholicism. As Catholics live under the "cursed state" defined by St. Thomas as being "without the fullness of God's special graces."

Our Fatima Curse is the absence of the Canonized Latin Mass Liturgy and the prevalence of the Bishops' "New Mass," which is (in Pope Paul VI's words–"a novelty," ***in se, not*** **a "Mass." Thus, it is devoid of grace and mercy. God's theophany of Tuy revealed the Mass as the Source of "Grace and Mercy" coming down from Heaven at a Latin Mass altar as the Blessed Trinity was shown in Crucifixion (with Holy Mary at the foot of the Cross) producing and bestowing Grace and Mercy via the Holy Sacrifice of Christ's Canonized Latin Mass. Tuy gives a very explicit picture of God's Salutary Will.**

Before considering the Third Revelation, note that *all of the Marian apparitions* to the Latin Patriarchate from Guadalupe (1513) on, concerned the Canonized Latin Mass. Each vision demanded that a chapel be built; or, occurred within a chapel or church, wherein the Canonized Latin Mass Rite was said (as happened with St. Catherine Laboure).

Obviously, the Third Revelation of Fatima must implicitly or explicitly concern the loss of "grace and mercy" or the loss of the Mass, within the Latin or Roman Patriarchate; as well as, the Liturgical Revolution within the Latin Patriarchate. This revelation was to be disclosed by 1960 (the inception of Vatican II) at the very latest. Had Pope John XXIII obeyed Our Lady, Vatican Two would have identified, suppressed and specifically condemned the sources of this liturgical revolution,which already had roots in the existential church. Instead, a demonic ecumenical spirit and the ambivalence of Vatican Two provided fertile soil for the growth of the "revolutionary" spirit of Vatican Two: the spirit of disobedience to Christ and His Church. The major expression of this spirit is to be found in the Bishops' "New Mass," which anti-Christ and anti-Church intent was manifested as early as 1962 with the Bishops' gross disobedience to Pope John XXIII's binding, *Veterum Sapientia,* which mandated Latin

in the seminary and the preservation of Latin in the Mass. We now wonder whether 1917; 1960 (the designated year of Fatima's third revelation); 1966 (the beginning of "New Masses;" or 1969 (the year of the "official imposition" of the Bishops' "New Mass") began the one hundred year reign of Satan predicted by Pope Leo XIII. Whatever may be the case, it is obvious that we now suffer the greatest misfortune ever perpetuated by clergymen: the deprivation of the Canonized Latin Mass.

Bishops' Revolution Under the Bishop of Rome

"It's a whole "new church" since Vatican Two–and I like it!"
[Words of "New Mass" lay ministers.]

The "New Mass" is the post-Vatican Two "liturgical baby" of the Bishops' Revolt (of the 20th century), which began in the1960's. I, myself, prove this. I was ordained on June 7, 1966, in a Canonized Latin Mass. Having said this my only Canonized Mass until my enlightenment in 1988, I had any number of the legion of "New Mass" texts at my disposal (in various dioceses throughout the world). For over three years, I was unimpeded by reigning Bishops to celebrate a

grossly illicit "novelty," using Pope Paul VI's word. Not one Bishop objected to my or my "confreres" use of alien, fake Mass liturgies. From 1966 until 1969, the "New Mass" was not only accepted, but promoted by Bishops.

Papal "reference" to (the use of) "New Mass" Liturgy did not first appear until October 1969, (more than three years after "New Mass" was an "episcopal *fait accompli"*). Obviously, as also previously noted by Fr. De Pauw, the Bishops revolted from their Christ-given vows to the Catholic Church well before October, 1969. Cardinal Ratzinger notes the fruits of their liturgical revolt:

> **"For them, the liturgy has degenerated into a 'show' in which attempts are made to make religion interesting with the help of fashionable trivialities or seductive maxims, which produce an ephemeral success among the group of liturgical designers..."**
>
> *The Liturgical Reform,* Mgr. Klaus Gamber, p. 6, "Foreword," Cardinal Ratzinger

---

"When good priests, in obedience to their bishops, will have sufficiently distanced themselves from what is divine and lost themselves in what is human, come to realize that they have been 'had,' it will be too late...Here is the episcopal crime committed against the Priesthood."

Abbe de Nantes, Ccr, n 25, p.9

The Big Lie

"We are not teachers of a doctrine born of the human mind, but we are in conscience bound to embrace and follow the doctrine which Christ Our Lord taught and which He solemnly commanded His Apostles and their successors to teach (Matt 28:19-20). Pope Pius XII, (1939-1958)

To impose their "New Mass," revolting Bishops told big lies–lies "born of the wicked imaginings and machinations of the human mind." Then, they demanded conformity or implementation. Remarkably, with the notable exception of Cardinal Ottaviani who perceived *in se* invalidity, few recognized and protested the gross invalidity of these new and strange novelties. However, God wills that if and when an individual "Holy Ordered Priest" comes to see that the "New Mass" is likely or "probably" invalid, he must cease and desist. A Priest is never allowed to use a *doubtfully valid* liturgical action regarding the Mass and confecting the sacraments.

It was in 1969, not long after the Bishops' attained their "New Mass" that the Bishops changed to their "new ordinal." According to the Pope Leo's Leonine principle, ordination defines service and vice versa. Invalid services "produce" invalid ordinations and vice versa. (See *Apostolicae Curae.*) ***Apostolicae Curae* forms**

the dogmatic basis for the conviction that both "New Mass" Service and "New Ordinal" are not valid, since, like the Anglican, they grossly violate the dogmatic *Quo Primum:*

> **We determine and order by this Our decree, to be valid in perpetuity, that *never shall anything be added to, omitted from or changed in this Missal...*** [Author's note: To act contrary to this dogma constitutes heresy and heresy invalidates.] **Specifically, do We warn all persons in authority, of whatever dignity or rank...and command them, as a matter of strict obedience, never to use or permit any ceremonies or *Mass prayers* other than the ones contained in this Missal."**
> *Quo Primum,* Pope St. Pius V, July 19, 1570, italics/brackets added.

"New Mass" Popes, Bishops and Priests suffer under the "Romans One Curse" (Rm 1:16-2:5)**. They not only sin, but call sin, virtue. Not only do they call sin, virtue, but impose it on others under the cloak of obedience. They reward those who agree with their sinning and also sin; and depose those who do not. Previous to Vatican Two, Bishops weakened their priests in seminary training by reducing Christ's Canonized Latin Mass Liturgy to a set of outdated, burdensome, legalistic words and deeds; and, by failing to transmit vital and inspiring notions, insights and aspects of the Canonized Mass [as presented in *Mystery of Faith* and *Latin Mass Prayers Explained*].**

Pope Paul VI
Founding Bishop of "New Mass"

"The Novus Ordo is a striking departure from the Catholic theology of the Holy Mass."
So stated the Cardinals' Commission of upper clergy and theologians to Pope Paul VI regarding that version of the Novus Ordo which was closer to being orthodox than the Novus Ordo English Liturgy.

Complicating the "theological picture" even more, one notes that, at Vatican Two, Pope Paul VI reduced himself to an episcopal role as he joined the Bishops' Revolt. He reduced himself to being merely "Bishop of Rome," under which title he signed the non-dogmatic "veiled platform statements" of Vatican Two, (which Council he decreed to be *non-dogmatic).* Despite his papal confession that the "New Mass" was a "novelty," Pope Paul VI surrendered the Canonized Latin Mass Liturgy "of priceless worth."

[Later, it was Pope John Paul II, because of his "excommunication" of Archbishop Marcel Lefebvre (famous for his attempt to hold and transmit the Canonized Latin Mass) who gave ignorant Catholics the impression that there was "something so wrong" with Christ's Canonized Latin Mass that Archbishop Lefebvre had to be excommunicated. One wonders why disobedient revolting "New Mass" Bishops were

not excommunicated by Pope Paul VI?]

The Bishops rejected Christ's liturgy in order to form their own apostate liturgy, based on the enthronement of man and the dethronement of God as exists in secular humanism, which is, *de facto,* the established religion of most western nations. One prays as he believes. *"We, more than others have the cult of man,"* said Pope Paul VI at the United Nations.

For the doctrine of faith as revealed by God has not been presented to men as a philosophical system to be perfected by human ingenuity; it was presented as a divine trust given to the bride of Christ to be faithfully kept and infallibly interpreted... any meaning of the sacred dogmas...once declared by holy Mother Church, must always be retained;...there must never be any deviation from that meaning on the specious grounds of a more profound understanding (see 83, can.3)**. 'Therefore, let there be growth...; but only within proper limits... the same doctrine... the same meaning... the same purport.'**

First Vatican Council, ch 4, DS no. 80

The Case Against the Bishops

> **"The clearest sign of God's anger and the most horrible punishment He can inflict upon this world is manifested when He permits His people to fall into the hands of clergy who are clergymen more in name than in deed." St. John Eudes**

The primary concern of every Catholic is (or should be) the "New Mass" produced, supported and implemented by the Bishops, including the Pope as Bishop of Rome. The *sensus et praxis fidelium* (what the Catholic faithful have always believed and done) did not demand that Christ's Mass be changed. The *sensus et praxis fidelium* clearly forbade and totally condemned such a liturgical aberration. The faithful did not create the liturgical problem with which Catholics are faced. The Bishops rejected the Catholic Mass. They abandoned the Catholic Religion. In as much as the existential church is apostate and not Catholic, the apostasy originates, and is forcibly implemented and confirmed by the Bishops.

The Bishops are revolting against Catholicism, especially Christ's Canonized Latin Mass! Holy Ordered Priests, ("ordered" at their ordination to "transubstantiate bread and wine into the Body and Blood of Christ," whose lives are dedicated to

celebrate Christ's Holy Mass), have been abolished by apostate Bishops (in the same way Protestant bishops abolished the Holy Ordered Priesthood). Before being abolished in 1970 or so, Holy Ordered Priests (as opposed to those episcopally commissioned to be presiders and episcopal collaborators) were first victimized in 1966.

I know! I was one of the last classes to be validly ordained in and for the Canonized Latin Mass (6/7/66). In fact, I had practiced saying the Canonized Latin Mass and was ordained by the Catholic Ordinal–yet, I never said a true Mass from June 8, 1966 until my retirement. Why? The Bishops "spiritually violated or raped me." By imposing the "New Mass," they deprived me of my ordination rite "to celebrate the Holy Sacrifice of the Mass for the living and the dead."

I reiterate that Pope Paul VI did not initiate the Liturgical Revolt, since, from 6/8/66 until the papal reference to a new service on 11/19/69 – (a period of three years) neither I, nor any of my priest colleagues were ever reprimanded (by even one Bishop) for saying a false, unapproved Mass-simulating liturgy. Why? We were already then, and still are, in the Bishops' Liturgical Revolt. And, in all fairness to Pope John XXIII, it must be noted, as reported by

Rev. Dr. Gommar de Pauw, that on February 22, the Feast of St. Peter's Chair, Pope John XXIII, in a most solemn ceremony, issued his *Veterum Sapientia:*

> **"In the full awareness of Our office and of Our authority, We decree and order ad Perpetuam Rei memoriam – in perpetuity," he said. "We will and command that this Our constitution remain firmly established and ratified notwithstanding anything to the contrary..." And that constitution said that Latin had to stay in the liturgy and that the bishops had the obligation to see to it that no one under their authority works for the elimination of the Latin from either the liturgy or the studies for the priesthood in our seminaries. That was 8 months before the Vatican Council opened. And the Pope made it clear that this was ad Perpetuam Rei memoriam "for all perpetuity, this must remain in the fullness of Our authority We make this decision." he said...**
>
> **And it was in that year, 1962, that a schismatic heretical, Conciliar sect of the Church in the United States of America was born. Why? Because regardless of the clear, solemn oath of Pope John XXIII, the majority of our American bishops refused to obey. I should know because I was there on the faculty at the time. And I had instructions from our Bishop in Baltimore NOT to implement the constitution from Rome. That's when I resigned."**

Rev. Dr. Gommar de Pauw, *Conciliar or Catholic?* 1967
www.traditio.com

The Bishops' Revolt from Bugnini's Mouth

> **"We were assured that as times changed, so must ritual...we were told a million lies and half truths."**
> *The Latin Mass,* Joseph Cardinal Ratzinger, Special Edition 1966

The Bishops' Liturgical Revolt centers on the "New Mass." Every time a Bishop allows and imposes a "New Mass" in his diocese, he recommits himself to the Liturgical Revolution, to apostasy within. The "liturgical buck" originates and is sustained by apostate Bishops within the existential church.

As Annibale Bugnini confesses, those who held sway, power and opportunity working in the Vatican and wherever opportunity prevailed, were enabled and empowered by the episcopal convocation of Vatican Two and the intricacy of its workings, to bring forth modernist ideas under the guise of church and liturgical "reform." Due to the fact that these ideas were "couched in traditional language," (albeit their conclusions deviated from all tradition) these Church-condemned postulations were cleverly woven through the Vatican bureaucracy; received the necessary episcopal vote; and, were episcopally approved for experimentation. (*The Reform of the Liturgy 1948–1975,* Annibale Bugnini, Preface, p. xxxiv, xxv)

Trust and Obey Us Bishops!

"The pontifical dignity can also be lost by falling into certain insanity..as well as, through manifest and notorious heresy."
Udalricus Beste, theologian

What often prevents individuals from seeing the obvious facts and arriving at the obvious conclusion–that "New Mass" liturgical services are conclusively invalid and sacrilegious–is the establishment's own perverted definition of "infallibility."Have you ever consulted a "New Mass" cleric regarding criticisms of the Bishops' "New Mass?" Naturally, the cleric first plays the "trust and obey us" card: "Trust us. God is with His Church. God would never allow us to lead you into error. Obey us." In effect, he says "We are infallible." To bolster their communal episcopal "infallibility" or to back up their "trust and obey us" ploy, Bishops invoke "papal infallibility." They claim that modern popes are infallible in allowing the "New Mass." Bishops lie! In his book *Introduction to the Spirit of the Liturgy* Cardinal Ratzinger writes:

"Following the Second Vatican Council, the idea was diffused that the Pope can do whatever he likes in regard to the liturgical matters...Consequently, the idea that the liturgy is something that precedes, and that it

cannot be 'made' on the basis of one's own judgment, has been lost in the West. In fact, it was not without reason that the First Vatican Council did not define the Pope as an absolute monarch. The First Vatican Council considered the Pope as the guarantor of obedience in regard to the word which was handed down: his authority is tied to the tradition of faith and this also applies to liturgical matters [...] The authority of the Pope is not unlimited; it is subject to holy tradition."
Introduction to the Spirit of the Liturgy, Cardinal Ratzinger, St. Paul Press

Chancellor Bismarck claimed that the First Vatican Council's declaration of papal infallibility had made the Pope a despot. In 1875, the German Bishops made a joint declaration regarding Bismarck's claim. They stated that:

1. **The Pope "is subject to Divine Revelation and is bound to the commandments which Jesus Christ gave to His Church."**

2. **"The Catholic Church is certainly not a society which accepts the immoral and despotic principle that the authority of the superior frees him unconditionally from his personal responsibility."**

3. **"Infallibility is a concept which encompasses exclusively the supreme magisterium of the Pope, and this is [...] linked to that which one finds in Sacred Scripture and Tradition; and, also, in the**

definitions which emanate from the Ecclesiastical Magisterium." Pope Pius IX praised the German Bishops for these "most excellent clarifications" which defended "the true sense of the First Vatican Council" against dangerous distortions. "We confirm them," he declared, "with the fulness of our apostolic authority."

4. **All this being said, surely it is time to start correcting all that which contradicts Holy Tradition in what was implemented following Vatican II!**

Catholic, "Si Si No No, 'Si Si' to Cardinal Ratzinger," Oct. 2002

None of the Bishops' "peculiar beliefs or liturgical practices"* are binding. They cannot be *objects of "infallible declaration."* They are anti-Christ and anti-Church; and, therefore, cannot be infallible. Infallibility of the Pope guarantees only that the divine assistance will prevent an infallible declaration, *ex cathedra,* of such apostasy. This is true in the present crisis beginning with Vatican Two, which Popes assured us was simply of a "pastoral" nature; and, not doctrinal, as were all the twenty other Ecumenical Councils. After Vatican Two, no Pope has written with full papal authority; and, *a fortiori,* no Pope has dogmatically decreed "anything new" (such as "New Mass"). Sensible theologians agree that papal infallibility has not established the Bishops' "New Mass." *De facto,

apostate prelates and "responsibly cooperative victims" are anathema (damned to Hell). So states the Catholic Church:

> **"If anyone shall say that the received [from Christ] and approved rites [specifically approved and spelled out by this Council] of the Catholic Church...may be changed by any pastor of the churches [Eastern or Roman Rite churches of the present or of the future, be these pastors, bishops or patriarchs] to other new ones: let him be anathema."**
>
> *De Sacramentis,* Canon 12, Council of Trent

All Heaven concurs! Anathema be! May those who reject Christ's Canonized Latin Mass and impose man's "New Mass" as being valid or canonized–be anathematized. What can be clearer than this? Recalling our serious obligation (expressed in the Oath Against Modernism and reflected by Vatican Council One) "to understand words as they are commonly understood," it should be obvious that Trent dogmatically confirmed the liturgical morals of the Canonized Latin Mass as given to us by Christ in Apostolic Tradition. Since Christ's Canonized Mass prevailed since the inception of the Church, are we not led to conclude that the Bishops' "New Mass" was instituted by Satan and implemented by "apostate Bishops?" Is it not the liturgy of the Second Beast (Apoc 13)**? Is it not "legion** (Mk 5:9)**?"**

“Infallibility” as Church-Defined

“The Holy Ghost was not promised to the successor of Peter for them to make a new doctrine known, but for them to maintain in a holy way, the revelation transmitted by the Apostles, that is, the Deposit of Faith.”
The Dogmatic Vatican Council One

“Rome” and the Pope are subject to “the Church of the past.” In fact, Rome and the Pope have a higher duty and responsibility before God (than ordinary Catholics) to be subject to “the Church of the past.” They must conform to Christ-given, Apostolic faith and morals (especially, liturgical morals) or lose authority to demand conformity. In other words, to be binding, every papal statement or command and every episcopal statement or command must always be evaluated in terms of “the Sacred Magisterium” (Catholic credenda) – the collection of those doctrines (or “whats”) which one must embrace and observe in order to be a faithful Catholic. In modern times, up until Vatican Two, “Rome” was in agreement with the Apostolic See (or the See of St. Peter, the Holy See).

In the Catholic Church Herself, every care must be taken that we may hold fast to that which has been believed everywhere, always and by all.
St. Vincent of Lerins, 450 A.D.

Chapter Six

BUGNINI'S ASSIGNMENT: CREATE "NEW MASS" TO CELEBRATE MAN

"Be careful! Father Bugnini is asking for this permission so that superiors will be faced with a *fait accompli.*"
The Reform of the Liturgy 1948-1975, Annibale Bugnini, p. xxvii

---

666 – 6 is the number of man (created on the sixth day). "666" is man "thriced" or the celebration of man enthroned. Such is the "New Mass" Liturgy's "native character and spirit." The spirit of this liturgy dethrones God and enthrones man (666).

***"Take away the Mass, take away the Church,"* said Martin Luther. The Bishops imitated Luther. In collusion with Bugnini, in Rome, they replaced the Christ-instituted Mass with a satanic counterfeit, reduced Catholicism (as to destroy it) and gave Satan his greatest victory–liturgical apostasy within. They replaced Christ's Canonized Mass with Satan's Abomination of Desolation: the unholy in the place of the Most Holy, where man (the sinner) is celebrated; Christ the Saviour (of sinful man) is "de-God-ed." The Bishops' "New Mass" has taken away His divinity, humanized Christ to be a "friend," a**

"brother," a man, the one who glories in and glorifies "holy humanity."

Satan is one of the most intelligent creatures "by nature" that God ever made, knowing how to manipulate man (as Genesis, ch 3 reveals.) Satan worked through select members of the uppermost clergy, creating "New Mass" and "new religion"–apostasy within! How did he do so?

Take into account the "happy spirit" of the sixties (1960's). **The logon of that time was "structural change; communal celebration, protests, love-fests, fist power and flower-power characterized the rebellious sixties. Satan, through Archbishop Bugnini and a host of other alleged "experts," created "New Mass" and "new religion" in the same spirit: "change structures to celebrate man" or to implement the "666 liturgy." Bugnini himself later described the implementation of his liturgical revolution as *"a major conquest of the Catholic Church."*** ("How the liturgy fell apart: the enigma of Archbishop Bugnini," Michael Davies, www.ad2000.com.au/articles/1989/jun1989p17_640.html

In the midst of these love fests, many clergy of the fifties and sixties emotionally hated the Latin Mass structure, mostly because they did not adequately know, nor firmly believe in the Canonized Latin Mass Prayers due to inadequate priestly formation.

The theology of the Canonized Latin Mass was cut off at its inception, as the clergy embraced "novelty," ascertaining daily as to whether or not each ritual or spiritual undertaking was presently "relevant."

The clergy shifted interest from God to "this world," emptying out convents, seminaries, even rectories as priests fled their vocational commitments, many to marry. This sixties' zeitgeist found its major expression and ongoing vital inspiration in the Bishops' Mass-simulating liturgies. Episcopal "fist-power" jerked away the old liturgical Mass structure. Bishops force-fed the faithful with new liturgical communal "love-fests" in place of the Canonized Latin Mass text.

Change and Community Celebration

It's rather simple. Change is mandated. Alleged "reigning experts" (pawns of Satan) determine "structural change" – in the "spirit of Vatican Two." Then, in disobedience to God's Will, willing, duped, ignorant, Bugnini-supporting Bishops implement (evil) decisions, insisting on uniformity and absolute obedience: "Obey and trust us (as we disobey Christ

and His Church). We [who are really apostates] are the apostles alive in your midst."

The "spirit" defined the action; *lex credendi* defined *lex orandi;* evil principles defined the Bishops' "New Mass": all in the name of "change." The old was removed, the new, ruthlessly installed. The spiritual yielded to the sensual. Sacred ritual and rubrics were replaced with joyful communal celebration. Man is celebrated in the "666 liturgy (cf. Ap 13):" Burdensome to modern man, liturgical structure was removed and discarded. Man had it easy and could now celebrate life, according to Bugnini:

> **"Liturgical actions and sacramentals...should increasingly become "celebration..." Attention is no longer focused on the minimum required for the validity of liturgical actions nor simply on their outward form...but on the congregation that has gathered to hear and respond to God's word, share in the sacrament, remember the Lord Jesus, and give thanks to God the Father, by whose great mercy 'we have been reborn to a living hope through the resurrection of Jesus Christ from the dead' (1Pet 1:3)."**
>
> *The Reform of the Liturgy,* 1948-1975Annibale Bugnini, p. 40

Salvation already possessed elicits communal rejoicing. *"We are a celebrating people,"* is the heresy of heresies! Satan's greatest victory is the "liturgization of presumption." As in Protestantism,

we are already saved by our belief in Christ. Thereby, any type of here and now Saving Action or (Christ) Mass is redundant and counterproductive to the community's ecumenical celebration of its sinfully presumed "Godliness."

Bugnini's "New Mass" believes that each man is saved by birth (cf. *Redemptoris Hominis,* the inaugural encyclical of Pope John Paul II). **Bugnini discarded Christ's liturgy as "the God-defined way to praise God" in order to impose his "New Mass" and "new religion"–the man-devised communal celebration of "being saved once and forever."** ***("Salvation is made present in liturgical celebration,"*** **states Bugnini.) Full and active participation of the laity is demanded as stated by the master.**

> **"Participation in the salvation which Christ has accomplished...is made present in liturgical celebrations. The song that is the liturgy kindles love of God in the hearts of the faithful and brings them to a full realization of his interventions in their behalf; it inspires them to tell others what they themselves have seen and contemplated, and to bear witness by their lives to what they have received through faith (see no. 10). The centrality of the liturgy must be kept in mind in teaching, catechetics, and pastoral practice...**
>
> **The very nature of the liturgy, as well as, the baptismal character that makes of the faithful "a chosen race, a**

royal priesthood, a holy nation, a people God has made His own to praise his wonders," requires that they be led to a "full, conscious, and active participation in liturgical celebrations" (no. 14). This participation is both their right and their duty. The full and active participation of all the people has been a special concern in the reform and promotion of the liturgy, for the liturgy is the primary and indispensable source from which the faithful can derive the Christian spirit. This thought has been the basic motive at work in the modern liturgical renewal and the conciliar documents."

The Reform of the Liturgy 1948-1975, Annibale Bugnini, p.41

The Fate of Vestiges

Disobey Church regulations and customs in order to change them! Revolt! For the Novus Ordo, (New Order) to come into being, structure must be changed. Each classical or traditional structure is like the human appendix. The appendix is a vestigal organ. It is tolerated as part of the body as long as it does not become active. So, also, with vestiges of true Mass. They are tolerated so long as they "do not come alive so as to threaten or devour any aspect of 'New Mass.'" Regarding "latin vestiges," it is noted that in spring, 2004, certain "messages from Rome"

indicate a growing possibility of granting great freedom to the use of latinized “New Masses” or other forms of “latin Masses.” Since the Bishops changed to “new ordinals,” (and it is likely that there are few validly ordained priests) are they now convinced that it is safe for the apostate “New Mass” to bring back Latin?

Some vestiges (such as partially “latinized Mass praying”) could be perverted to conform to the “666 spirit of disobedience.” Some vestiges can be demonized, as for example, modern “versions” of the Bible have been perverted by modern scripture scholars to remove the “God-given sting,” leaving “generalities, pleasantries and unresolvable confusion.”

After perverting Bible reading, “New Mass” fabricators went on to remove Catholicism from the Mass Prayers. The master satanic disciple, Bugnini, pledged himself and a host of others (over 200 would be needed worldwide) to accomplish this task by a double-pronged attack: impose the satanic will of the experts through cooperating Bishops upon ‘hyped-up” communities, being so “cocky” as to impose demonic change (paradoxically–as predicted by Pope St. Pius X) in the name of tradition (as selectively perverted by reigning experts). Bugnini tells us:

“The directives and principles set down in the Constitution amount to a general mobilization of the entire Church. The pastors of local Churches, along with all their pastoral workers, are urged to start the process of educating the faithful in the liturgy, familiarizing them with the Scriptures, and getting them actively involved in the celebration through listening and singing and through acclamations, prayers, and responses. In addition, they are to begin the work of translating the liturgical books; this is a completely new field, full of difficulties and responsibilities.

...The reform will be a labor of sensitive, intelligent renewal, in which ‘elements that, with the passage of time, came to be duplicated or were added with but little advantage are now to be discarded; other elements that have suffered injury through accident of history are now, as may seem useful or necessary, to be restored to the vigor they had in the tradition of the Father’ (no. 50). It will be a work of simplification, so that the rites may radiate what the Constitution calls ‘a noble simplicity’ and be ‘short, clear, and unencumbered by useless repetitions; they should be within the people’s powers of comprehension and as a rule not require much explanation’ (no. 34). It will be a work that concentrates on essentials and has a useful pastoral purpose.

These various areas of activity will require a considerable effort and will bring the Church’s best powers into play for a number of years. Neither the revision of the liturgical books nor their translation can

be simply improvised. Nor can the training of the faithful be accomplished by a few brief instructions, but only by a slow, persevering, intelligent, and prolonged effort. The principles set down by the Council will be reduced to practice in a gradual process. The road will be long and difficult, but also sure. At the end the Church will have a renewed liturgy.....”

Reform of the Liturgy 1948-1975, Annibale Bugnini, p. 48

Who Was Annibale Bugnini?

Annibale Bugnini was born in Civitalla de Lego, Italy, in 1912; was ordained a Vincentian in 1936, spending ten years as a parish priest. Bugnini himself documents his part in the undermining of the Church. This satanically inspired prelate devised a “People’s Mass” which would replace Christ’s Catholic Mass. Bugnini fabricated the “New Mass,” guided its passage successfully through the hierarchical structures, and designed a master plan (See above quote.) of coordination to enable the Bishops to implement “New Mass” worldwide. (See *The Reform of the Liturgy: 1948–1975.)*

1948 – Secretary to Pope Pius XII’s Commision for Liturgical Reform;

1956 – consultor to the Sacred Congregation of Rites;

1957 – Professor of Sacred Liturgy in the Lateran University;

1960 – Secretary to the Preparatory Commission for the Liturgy of Vatican Council II; his papers, referred to as the "Bugnini schema," accepted by plenary session Jan. 13, 1962; despite opposition of Cardinal Gaetano Cicognani, President of the Commission, the Liturgy Constitution passed schema substantially identical to the Bugnini schema;

1962 – abrupt dismissal from chair at Lateran University for reasons never disclosed and was the only secretary of a preparatory commission not confirmed as secretary of the conciliar commission; occurred under Pope John XXIII;

1966 – Secretary to the Preparatory Commission under Pope Paul VI; Commission ended the existence of the Consilium, making it part of the Congregation of Divine Worship;

1972 – consecrated Archbishop;

1974 – boasted that the reform of the liturgy had been a "major conquest of the Catholic Church;" [Note: Bugnini himself validates the facts in this book.]

1975 – abruptly dismissed, his congregation dissolved and merged with the Congregation for the Sacraments; became Apostolic Nuncio in Iran. It is said that Pope Paul VI dismissed Bugnini, believing him to be a Mason, which Bugnini denied; although the Vatican refused to explain the dismissal, the charge was never denied by the Vatican. In his article, Michael Davies explains further:

"The sequence of events was as follows. A Roman priest of the very highest reputation came into possession of what he considered to be evidence proving Mgr. Bugnini to be a Mason. He had this information placed in the hands of Pope Paul VI by a cardinal, with a warning that if action were not taken at once he would be bound in conscience to make the matter public. The dismissal and exile of the Archbishop followed."

"How the liturgy fell apart: the enigma of Archbishop Bugnini,
Michael Davies
www.ad2000.com.au/articles/1989/jun1989p17_640.html

The above quote is a sensible explanation for the situation Catholics have endured in Christ's Church during the period of Annibale Bugnini's career and shows good reason for Bugnini's dismissal from Rome. Bugnini's own words bring one to the sad realization that the Bishops and religious educators were in collusion with this plan. Their actions were definite and deliberate. Where is the strategy to depose such apostate Bishops?

~~~~~~

"We ask the Holy Father to PLEASE be a Pope; to act like a Pope; to stand on his own two feet; and to give us loyal traditionalist Catholics the satisfaction of being able once more to say: "Rome has spoken and all Catholics will obey!" That's what we asked him to do."

Rev. Dr. Gommar de Pauw, *Conciliar or Catholic?* 1967

~~~~~~

Now Is the Time for Bishops to Repent: Bring Back the Canonized Latin Mass

Having personally lived through the 60's Revolt, watching this Bugnini-orchestrated strategy "happening" before my very eyes: "adult education" classes to reduce faithful Catholics to apostates; children led to spiritual suicide in "sex education;" one can only marvel: at such an undertaking; at what type of persons would "do this"-- raise fists to God; at the precision success; all the while mourning one's time uselessly spent reporting to hierarchs, which complaints one now feels, was "music to their very ears," signs of their demonic success.

Having Bugnini explain that it was a strategy, a plan, a deliberate execution in collusion with the Bishops and religious educators to rid the Church of Christ's Salutary Holy Mass and Religion, one can only gnash one's teeth in frustration at such a demonism. One now directs a just anger toward the Bishops who revolted and "did this"– all of them–since there is not one Bishop who has remained truly faithful in his office, kept only the Canonized Latin Mass!

Let us have a Rosary Crusade to petition our Blessed Mother to return Christ's Holy Mass and Religion to each parish church–to depose all unfaithful Bishops! Where is one Bishop who will repent? Where is the strategy, the precision plan, the collusion to "put it all back"–to repair that which they have stolen?! And what of the souls who are damned? Bishops must be held accountable ! They cannot blame priests!

Victim of the Bishops' Revolution

Preponderance of Evidence
Christ-Given Salutary Truth

Christ instituted the Mass.

His Church Canonized the Mass to be "as Christ instituted" it to be–in perpetuity–forever–period!

As regards the Bishops' "New Mass," Pope Paul VI's own words refer to "New Mass" as a "novelty."

The plenitude of the constant teaching of the Catholic Church (only a fraction of which appears in these pages) constitutes the preponderance of evidence which shows that "New Mass" cannot be valid.

This book is not meant to reflect evidence as in a court case, but, rather, to bring to the fore truths of the Christ-instituted Holy Mass and Catholic Church and the mandate from Christ to uphold (but never change) Christ-given Salutary Truth.

Pope St. Pius X (1903-1914)

Giuseppe Melchior Sarto (1835-1914)
Pope Saint Pius X, Canonized in 1954 by Pope Pius XII

Pope St. Pius X is the only pope since Pope St. Pius V (1566-1572) to have been canonized as a saint of the Church. In 1907, his Holy Office published the famous decree *Lamentabili Sane,* in which 65 propositions drawn from the works of Modernist writers, were condemned. He himself issued the encyclical, *Passcendi,* in which he outlined the errors of Modernism–the cult of "Man." As such, it is the source and summation or "synthesis of all heresies." This sainted pope suppressed and removed from the seminaries and universities Modernist teachers. In 1910, he required all priests to take the Oath Against Modernism.

www.traditio.com/papal/piusx.htm

Chapter Seven

BUGNINI'S "PEOPLE'S MASS" AND "ITS FACILITATOR"

"Participation in the salvation which Christ has accomplished...is made present in liturgical celebration." *The Reform of the Liturgy, 1948-1975,* Bugnini,p.41

The Bishops' "New Mass" teaches that all are to participate in "New Mass" of "salvation accomplished." This salvation is accomplished (not by Christ's Holy Sacrifice) but, somehow and somewhat, by the people's liturgical celebration itself. In communal joy, the whole world ecumenical community (in abstract) and now, this local community celebration takes the place of Christ's Holy Mass, recalling their "once and forever over with salvation."

Holy Supper Sacrifice, "in its true Catholic sense," has been rejected by the Bishops' "New Mass." This ritual, celebrated by community (not by a Holy Ordered priest) cannot in any manner be construed as "Mass." Community celebrates its presumed "God-ness" in various Mass-simulating liturgical settings.

Unlike Christ's Canonized Latin Mass, the People's "New Mass" does not focus on Christ as "sacrificially and sacramentally present" among them because of the Consecration; or, because of the priest's unique Holy Ordered power; or, because of Holy Sacrifice; but only, "by–in–and– through" the "gathering together" of the people of God who communally celebrate their "God-ness." As they sing their "gathering song," they presume the Resurrected Christ is in their community; He is in each individual; He is everywhere, but nowhere in a unique way--such as the Tabernacle or the Eucharist. He is not here "in or from" the Holy Sacrifice. Thus, the laity proclaim, define and "make relevant:" *"Christ has died; Christ is risen; Christ will come again!"* Christ is not here mystically/ sacramentally in Holy Sacrifice and Holy Sacrament.

The people themselves boldly proclaim that "New Mass" is not valid; it is "null and void; Christ is not "sacrificially or sacramentally" present here. "Christ has died. [Christ does not come upon altars from 'here and now' Holy Sacrifice.] Christ is risen and will come again." Christ is not here mystically nor sacramentally.

The people are here. Empowered by and in community, they celebrate themselves as "Christ."

Power, love, honor and glory to man–to each "Christ-ed" human. Each is saved by birth. Christ is in all. Therefore, celebrating oneself and community is celebrating the Christ in everyone. Empowered people celebrate their very own "God-ness!" Power to the people: "We live and Christ lives in us. This we celebrate in liturgy."

Faithful Catholics admit that only one human person is sinless. Only Mary is *in se* with the Lord and the Lord with her. The rest are sinners in dire need of being saved by and "taken into" Christ's Holy Sacrifice. Fundamentalist or evangelical Protestants agree that we are sinners in dire need of Christ, Saviour. However, those attending "New Mass," although that they may suffer from "bad form or mental kinks," are already and certainly "in Christ." This, they celebrate. They celebrate the people, the community!

Repentant sinners pray the Mass so as to be taken into Christ's Salutary Oblation–so as to be with the Lord, to receive and be taken into Holy Communion. Just as Holy Sacrament is born from Holy Sacrifice, so, in a similar way, do the just believe that they are taken into Christ. The just are born "of and into" the Realization of the Saving Will of God, the Holy Sacrifice of the Mass. It is "paradoxically

praiseworthy" that, quite consistent with their heretical holdings, "New Mass" facilitators ("ordained" to be "collaborators," presently still called "priests") are specifically and purposely not ordained to celebrate Mass, but to receive the gifts of the people of God, who do "celebrate Mass." They are merely presiders over the people's celebration of "New Mass," who can no longer clearly or validly claim to be Christ-priests who mystically/ sacramentally "re-present the Realization of God's Saving Will into the (here and now).

Why not? Purposely, they were not ordained to be such. With malice aforethought, as inspired by Bugnini, the Bishops (like their Anglican counter-parts) deliberately employ a bastardized ordination rite. The Bishops' "new ordinal" has been so changed as to lead one (such as Pope Leo XIII) to conclude that a Christ-instituted, traditional church "Holy Ordering" no longer exists or can exist within the Bishops' "New Mass" Liturgy. (See *Apostolicae Curae,* Pope Leo XIII's dogmatic "invalidaton of Anglican Orders and Masses;" Cardinals Ottaviani and Bacci's *Critical Studies,* 1969. See *Abbot & Me On Liturgy,* MAETA.) **Why does the upper clergy, in defiant disobedience of the Catholic Church, reject Ordination and Mass rituals which are "certainly valid and effective" in order to substitute rituals which *could not possibly be valid or effective?***

Perhaps, part of the reason could be found in Cardinal Baum's remarks (while still a Monsignor) that Anglicans, Lutherans and Taize Communities helped determine the nature of the Liturgical Revolution at Vatican Two. He said:

> **"They are not simply there as observers, but as consultants as well, and they participate fully in the discussions on Catholic liturgical renewal. It wouldn't mean much if they just listened, but they contribute."**
> Msgr. W. Baum, Detroit News, 6/7/67, as quoted by Leo Darroch, "The Development of the Mass Since 1960, 5/3/1995, www.latin-mass-society.org/leomass.htm

---

"The fashion... of saying Mass facing the people began in 1965...in imitation of the Protestant services. The Vatican sent out instructions saying that these Masses were not approved by the Holy See. These, like most things nowadays, were simply ignored. The disobedience and anarchy quickly spread and before you could blink an eye everyone was doing it. And why? Because Vatican II said so. If you are going to tell a lie, you may as well make it a big one. I will repeat, there is no binding Church law which states that sanctuaries have to be changed in the way that they all have been. Indeed, the situation is quite nonsense..."
Leo Darroch, "The Development of the Mass Since 1960 (What Vatican II Really Said)
www.latin-mass-society.org/leomass.htm

Pope John XXIII Decrees *Veterum Sapientia*

Eight months before opening Vatican Council II, after being warned that the Modernists would attack the Holy Mass, Pope John XXIII convoked his Cardinals within reasonable distance of Rome, and in solemn fashion, in St. Peter's Basilica, issued his Apostolic Constitution,, in which he declared that there was no council nor any bishop that could touch the traditional Latin Liturgy. On February 22, 1962, Pope John XXIII, in his *Veterum Sapientia* stated:

> **"In the full awareness of Our Authority, we decree and order ad Perpetuam Rei memoriam–(in perpetuity) ...We will and command that this Our Constitution remain firmly established and ratified notwithstanding anything to the contrary..."Pope John XXIII**
>
> **[The Pope made it clear... this was...for all perpetuity, this must remain in the fullness of Our Authority... We make this decision...]**
>
> **[Pope John said that Latin had to stay in the liturgy and that the Bishops had the obligation to make certain that no one under their authority worked for the elimination of Latin from the liturgy or from seminary studies for the priesthood]...**

Rev. Dr. Gommar de Pauw, *Conciliar or Catholic?* 1967

Chapter Eight

THE CANONIZED LATIN MASS: THEOLOGY STOPPED AT ITS INCEPTION

Unlike Vatican Two which was dominated by apostate alleged experts, Trent was determined by faithful bishops. For example, reflecting the fact that Mass theology is only at its beginning, not its culmination, the debate arose as to which was the Holy Sacrifice–the Supper or Calvary.

In discussing the Mass (at Trent) the Bishop of Bitonto introduced the thought that "Christ did not offer Himself at the Supper because His death would have been in vain, the Supper Sacrifice would have sufficed to reconcile us to God." The Bishop of Lodi counteracted this speculation in one statement: "The Sacrifice of the Supper and of the Cross is the same." [These facts are given by Fr. de la Taille in his *Mystery of Faith,* op. cit.]

Without a doubt, Martin Luther, as well as, Pope Paul VI, Bugnini, et al, "reformed" the liturgy, for religious determination or for religious purposes. Both the Protestant and the Bishops' "New Mass" movements rejected Catholic theology, which holds Holy Mass as being the Holy Sacrifice presented to us

here and now in a mystical/ sacramental way. Indeed, these man-made religions reject the Mass as instituted by Christ (as salutary Offering and Oblation) and canonized by His Church.

At this point, it is necessary to recollect two things. First, we are dealing with "the Most Holy, the Sacred Salutary Heart of Christ, the Heart of the one and only religion by which one can be saved from Hell; Christ's ever New and Eternal Living Will and Testament [the formula to effect that which was given by Christ to His Apostles between His Resurrection and Ascension and which essential formula was canonized within Apostolic Times by the *sensus et praxis fidelium]* and comes to us in the Latin Rite as the Canonized Latin Mass Text.

Secondly, Catholicism distinguishes the One Holy Sacrifice as "realized" at the Holy Supper; at every properly said Canonized Mass; and, as "realized and actualized" once and forever unrepeatably at Calvary. We do so in light of the dogmatic Tridentine resolution:

> **For the Victim is one and the same, the same now offering by the ministry of priests, Who once offered Himself on the Cross, the manner of offering alone being different. In other words, although there are as many sacrifices as there are offerings, at the same time there does exist a real oneness between the Mass and the Cross, by reason of the Victim which is offered (i.e. Christ).** The dogmatic Council of Trent

In the light of Catholic history or Reality, the "New Mass" is Satan's greatest victory. It is the existential termination of our only Salutary Necessity and God's Greatest Gift to sinful men. These statements are proven, not with a few proofs, but with the totality of Christ's Apostolic and Church teaching; not with superficial proofs, but with the totality of absolute Truth, which go to the heart of the Bishops' Liturgical Apostasy. To reject the conclusion that 'New Mass" is "null and void" or invalid, one must refute each and every one of the "proofs" which are presented in the rest of this book, proofs which consist of the dogmatic teaching of the Roman Catholic Church from Apostolic Times.

Within the Parameters of Theological Freedom

Can a faithful Catholic have the conviction that "New Mass" is not valid? By what right does any Catholic do so?

A Catholic must do so in good conscience by the very fact that Truth must be upheld. After the fact of apostate Bishops having replaced Christ's Holy Sacrifice and Sacrament with an apostate "New

Mass," by means of disobedience "on the very altar of Christ's obedience unto death," faithful Catholics are faced with the threat of being labelled "in schism" for merely posing the question as to whether or not the apostate "New Mass" is valid, so imperious and devoted to "obedience to themselves and their error" have the Bishops become.

In these times of prevailing theological incompetence and rampant theological perversion, it seems necessary to make a "belabored" clarification of my fiducial position (which is now, by God's grace, my personal fiducial conviction which I do not legislate as being inter-subjectively binding). A knowledge of and belief in *semper ubique idem* Catholic faith and liturgical morals (as lived, taught and clarified by the faithful within and consistent with Apostolic Times) leads me and "an ever-increasing number of faithful Catholics" to conclude that "New Mass" as imposed by post-Vatican Two Bishops is "null and void" or not valid. This book reflects my personal theological opinion, expressed within the parameters of theological freedom and discussion.

~~~~~~
~~~~~~

PART TWO

EVALUATING

THE "NEW MASS"

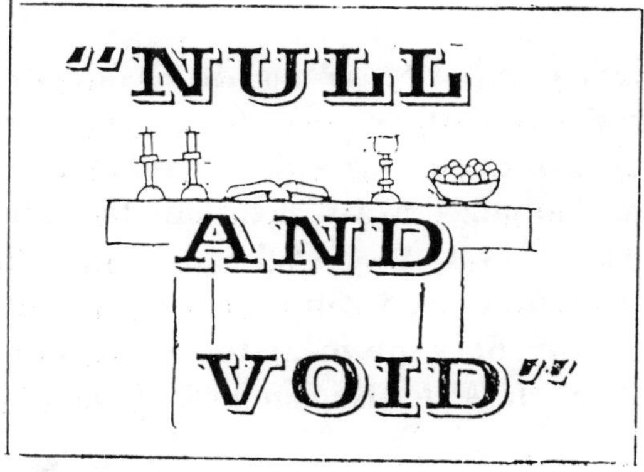

"The liturgical reform ... do not be deceived, this is where the [Bishops'] revolution begins."
Msgr. Dwyer, Archbishop of Birmingham, Chairman of the Episcopal Synod, 1970

The Anglican "New Mass" has the basic eight words of consecration and other words (of the consecration and offertory) which are far more in agreement with the Catholic Canonized Mass Text than does the Bishops' "New Mass;" yet, the Anglican "New Mass" was dogmatically decreed "null and void" or invalid. Consequently, does this mean that the Bishops' Novus Ordo "New Mass" is also conclusively invalid?

Chapter Nine

CRITERIA TO EVALUATE THE "NEW MASS"

The Novus Ordo ("New Mass") is like a platypus. The "New Mass" is a strange new creation. It is heretical, apostate, new age, protestant, masonic, anti-Christ and anti-Church.

---

valid–That which is necessary to produce the desired [Christ-instituted, Christ-given] effect: that action of a priest which is spiritually effective.

licit–That which is permitted by law, whether civil or ecclesial. Often distinguished from valid, to express what the law prescribes or allows, as distinct from what is necessary to produce the desired effect. Lawful, allowed, permitted.
Pocket Catholic Dictionary, John A. Hardon, S.J., Image Books, NewYork, 1980

Unlike its "better sister," the Anglican Liturgy, the Bishops' "New Mass" liturgizes and forms an apostate and heretical church body within the skeleton or shell of the true Church. Initially, many priests sensed this radical religious transformation and "voted their discontent with their feet." Within five years of the imposition of the "New Mass," the

number of priests decreased 50% from 413,000 to 243,000 *(Holy See Statistics).*

"New Mass" is so radically anti-Christ, that statisticians have not been led to formulate the big questions so as to properly assess the fruits of "New Mass." How many believe in Hell as "possible for them?" How many believe in Christ as the One and Only Saviour? How many believe in the salutary need to be virtuous and to do penance? How many believe in sin? How many believe in the Mass and Sacraments as instituted by Christ? How many believe in the Holy Sacrifice of the Mass, as the only way to be saved from eternal Hell? How many believe that each valid Mass must be the "Holy Ordered" mystical/sacramental "re-doing" of the Holy Supper Sacrifice; or, it is sacrilegious?

Is the legion (the various members of the set of ever-mutating "New Mass" Liturgies) valid or invalid? In the light of the dogmatic *Apostolicae Curae,* what is the criteria for "invalidity?"

Pope Leo XIII's Leonine Principles given in his dogmatic *Apostolicae Curae* (as expounded in this book) give us the Canonized Latin Mass Text from *"Suscipe Sancte Pater..."* through *"Per Ipsum..."* as our standard of judgment. The nature of the words

added to, modified or taken away from the Mass Text Standard (the Canonized Latin Mass Text) indicates the religious change that is made. The Council of Trent dogmatized the belief that these words could not be perfected. There was no justifiable reason to change the wording of the Mass; and, therefore, since the "New Mass" texts made deliberate and significant changes in the Canonized Latin Mass Text, one must conclude that "New Mass" is a serious rejection of Catholicism and the establishment or expression of a false religion and is "null and void" or invalid.

The Abbot & Me On Liturgy **[written by Abbot Gasquet (the author of *Apostolicae Curae* for Pope Leo) and myself] presents the mind and heart of *Apostolicae Curae* and applies this to both "New Masses" (Anglican and the Bishops' "New Masses"). In this book, this comparison is repeated and expanded, especially in the comparison of the offertory and consecration prayers of "New Masses," the Anglican and the Catholic liturgies.**

By Church Dogma Invalid

> **"I swear to Almighty God and the Saviour Jesus Christ that I will keep whatever has been revealed through Christ and His Successors and whatever the first councils and my predecessors have defined and declared."** Pope St. Agatho (678-681) Papal Oath

By church dogma, to be a Catholic one must believe that Christ instituted the Mass. How binding is this Christ-instituted Church-canonized Latin Rite Mass Text?

In the light of the dogmatic decision made by *Apostolicae Curae,* a Catholic is led to conclude that (within and for the Roman Rite) the Canonized Latin Mass Text is so binding that any deliberate and religiously significant departure from these Christ-given and Church-canonized words renders the Mass–like the Sacrament of Baptism–"null and void" or totally invalid! Catholics believe so. Catholics believe so in the "dogmatic light of *Apostolicae Curae.*"

Finally, recall that the Church-defined (dogmatically established) criteria for papal pronouncement of (or pastoral emphasis on) any item of faith or morals being infallible, was spelled out by the dogmatic decrees of the First Vatican Council (the last dogmatic Church Council). These criteria were

clearly and explicitly met by the dogmatic decrees of Trent and Quo Primum, whereby the Latin Mass Liturgy Text was "word for word" irrevocably canonized in perpetuity for the Latin Rite. Therefore, even prior to the writing of and, by the application of *Apostolicae Curae,* the Church expected the faithful to unhesitatingly conclude to the invalidity of the Anglican "New Ordinals" and "New Mass." This is stated in the beginning of the ever-binding *Apostolicae Curae:*

> Hence, it must be clear to everyone that the controversy lately revived had already been definitely settled by the Apostolic See, and that it is to the insufficient knowledge of these documents that we must, perhaps, attribute the fact that any Catholic writer should have considered it still an open question.
> *Apostolicae Curae,* No. 22, Pope Leo XIII.

Today, as then, the Church of Christ wonders how anyone could possibly consider the question of the invalidity of "New Mass" an open question, since the very principles of any "New Mass" were already determined. Obviously, from the Church's dogmatic teachings and practice, "New Mass" is invalid. The Apostolic See has spoken!

Conclusively Invalid

"I vow to change nothing of the received Tradition and nothing thereof I have found before me guarded by my God-pleasing predecessors; to encroach upon, to alter, or to permit any innovation therein..." Pope St. Agatho (678-681) Papal Oath

A careful and unprejudiced study of "New Mass" (for example, a study unbiased by blind and blinding obedience to, and trust of, dysfunctional, disobedient, existential church authorities) will inevitably lead a Catholic to see that the "New Mass" is "conclusively invalid." What does "conclusively invalid" mean? "Conclusively invalid" means that the "New Mass" is invalid as a legalistic conclusion: the "New Mass" cannot be valid in the light of Church teachings.

▲ **"Conclusively invalid" also means that, from studying the words (and rituals) within "New Mass" Novus Ordo Liturgy, one is led (as were those who produced *Apostolicae Curae* regarding the Anglican "New Mass") to conclude that the Bishops' "New Mass" is "similarly" invalid.**

▲ **Our times are similar to the times of the Arian Heresy (which denied that Christ is divine); when St. Jerome assures us that 90% or more of the bishops embraced the Arian Heresy. Then, as now, the existential church is dysfunctional and**

the essential, *semper ubique idem* church is purely Catholic. Most churchmen were wrong then (and most churchmen are wrong now) while the Church itself remained correct (and now remains correct): Jesus is God, in spite of what 99.9% of Bishops do; or even, in spite of what they may believe, teach and implement now, as in the past. Again, the Church remains correct: Christ's Canonized Latin Mass is the only canonized "licit and valid" Mass of the Latin Rite. By imposing conclusively invalid "New Mass," Mass-simulating liturgies, Bishops come up against dogmatic Church teachings. They embrace fundamental heresy. Thereby, they become apostates.

A major motivating force behind the Bishops' "New Mass" is its dedication to ecumenism. This demonic spirit is "anti-Trent." To be anti-Trent, is to be an apostate. The Bishops' "New Mass" liturgy is their liturgical expresion of such apostasy. As such, like the Anglican, it cannot be valid as a Mass. Bugnini himself described the "New Mass" Liturgy as *"a major conquest of the Catholic Church"* and, in effect, a "protestant liturgy." Fr. Braga, Bugnini's assistant, assured us that their liturgical creation resulted from "a revision of doctrinal reality." He also assured us that "New Mass" was Protestant. These remarks confirm our contention that the Bishops' rejected the true faith and embraced evil "Second Beast ecumenism."

Practical Theological Observations

"I vow...to cleanse all that is in contradiction to the canonical order, should such appear...." Pope St. Agatho, (678-681) Papal Oath

▲ **Barring the impossible, a Catholic is led to believe that "New Mass" is invalid. "The impossible" would be that a pope issues a *Quo Primum* for "New Mass." However, a pope cannot do so, since he cannot refute the dogmatic teaching that Christ instituted, and the Church irrevocably canonized, the Canonized Latin Mass Text.**

▲ **According to St. Thomas, the people's (or one of the congregation's) good intention will not make an invalid Mass into a valid one. Such an intention or "good will" does not validate the Eucharist. Because "one may think that Christ is present at this Mass and 'in the host'" does not make it so; or, put another way, does not make that which is invalid "valid."**

- **The minister's (or even the validly ordained priest's) good intention cannot make objectively valid an otherwise objectively invalid rite.** (See *Summa Theologica,* I-II 20.2.)

- **Once an ordained priest adequately perceives the heretical character of the "New Mass," his good intention cannot compensate for the serious offenses against the Godhead due to the nature of these "New Mass" rituals which *in se* presume, imply, contain or "effect" heresy** (Summa Theologica, I-II 20.2). **In other words, a truly good and well-intentioned priest cannot and will not say a "New Mass" Prayer Service (which is not a valid "Mass") since "New Mass" is evil by design. As written, the "New Mass" texts constitute a liturgical sacrilege unto invalidity.**

> **"It is said in the Acts of the Apostles: 'One ought to obey God rather than man.' Therefore, were a pope** [or bishop] **to command anything against...**[significant customs of] **the Church...he ought not to be obeyed.'"** (Summa de Ecclesia, 1489)Juan Cardinal DeTorquemada, O.P., (1388-1468); uncle of the Grand Inquisitor; officially designated theologian of the Council of Basel/ Florence; given by Pope Eugenius IV the title, Defender of the Faith.

~~~~~~~~~~~~~~~~~~~~~ **...That 'form'...cannot be considered...sufficient for the Sacrament which omits what it ought essentially to signify....#27 The Sacrament of Order and the true sacerdotium of Christ were utterly eliminated from the Anglican rite, and hence, the sacerdotium is in no wise conferred truly and validly in the episcopal consecration of the same rite, ...therefore, the episcopate can in no wise be valid and validly conferred by it, and this the more so because among the first duties of the episcopate is that of ordaining ministers for the Holy Eucharist and sacrifice...#29**

Being fully cognizant of the necessary connection...between 'the law of believing and the law of praying,' under a pretext of returning to the primitive form, they corrupted the Liturgical Order...to suit the errors of the reformers...There is no mention of the sacrifice, of consecration.... # 30 In vain has been the contention...that the said Ordinal can be understood and interpreted in a sound and orthodox sense... and thus...any words in the Anglican Ordinal which lend themselves to ambiguity, cannot be taken in the same sense as they possess in the Catholic rite...#31

A person...who has correctly used the requisite matter and form to effect and confer a sacrament is presumed for that very reason to have intended to do (intendisse) what the Church does...But...if the rite be changed, with the manifest intention of introducing another rite...and of rejecting what the Church does, and what, by institution of Christ, belongs to the nature of the Sacrament, then it is clear that, not only is the necessary intention wanting to the Sacrament, but that the intention is adverse to and destructive of the Sacrament....#33

This matter, although already decided, had been by certain persons... supposed that they possessed the Sacrament and effects of Orders, where these are nowise to be found...#35 Wherefore...we pronounce and declare that ordinations carried out according to the Anglican rite have been, and are absolutely null and utterly void....#36

We decree that these letters and all...contained therein shall not be... impugned or objected to by reason...of defect...of subreption or of obreption of our intention, but are and shall be always valid and in force and shall be inviolably observed both juridically and otherwise, by all of whatsoever degree and preeminence, declaring null and void anything ...contrariwise attempted, whether wittingly or unwittingly, by any person whatsoever, by whatsoever authority or pretense all things to the contrary notwithstanding....#40 Pope Leo XIII, *Apostolicae Curae* ~~~~~~~~~~~~
~~~~~~~~~~~~~~~~~~~~~

Chapter Ten

POPES ARE OPPOSABLE BISHOPS DEPOSABLE

"To the Catholic, who realized all that the Mass meant, how it was the center of his religion and the sublime Christ-bestowed Sacrifice–it was a point of honor and conscience to imperil fortune and even life for so sacred heritage."
Abbot (Cardinal) Gasquet, 1913, author of *Apostolicae Curae,* which condemned the New Anglican Order.

[For Catholics who wish to conform to Cardinal Gasquet's sentiments, see MAETA's Guidelines for Going Outside the Church for Mass and Confession and Fr. Morrison's *Directory of Traditional Latin Masses and Resource Book.* See also www.maeta.com and www.traditio.com]

The *in se* invalid "New Mass" some argue, in effect, becomes valid by being "Church law." First of all, we note that churchmen, including popes, can be wrong (and, thereby, are "opposable") in their "non-infallible:" pronouncements, decrees, policies legislations and "tolerations." This fact was illustrated at the "Joan of Arc" trial. At a crucial point in her trial, the great theologian, Joan, gave good advice for the faithful in our times. She agreed to obeying church authorities *conditionally: "provided that Our Lord is first served!"*

So must today's Catholics, in like manner, obey church authorities. Catholics cannot obey them as they impose the "New Mass" upon us. Why? Our Lord is not thus served! Only God is to be obeyed unconditionally. Only Jesus Christ, the Son of God, is God; and, as God, commanded His Christ-priests to do that Mass which He taught them to say (during the time between His Resurrection and Ascension), the Mass of Apostolic Tradition, the Canonized Latin Mass or Eastern Mass Ritual. *"Do this to effect the doing in Memoriam."*

"New Mass" is diametrically opposed to the Mass. "New Mass" is not Catholic. It is the liturgy which defines and expresses Newchurch, an apostasy from Catholicism.

Catholics obey living authorities (as St. Joan attested) provided that Our Lord is "first served." When confronted with churchmen who insisted that God spoke as "these" churchmen decided and not as God decreed, Joan opted for Christ's "Church of all time" over their church. Her historically recorded words apply to our times: *"It would seem that Christ and His [existential] church should be one. Why do you [wicked churchmen] make a difficulty where there should be no difficulty?"* Why have wicked Bishops imposed "New Mass?"

Apostate Bishops have purged their churches of Christ, Holy Sacrifice and Holy Sacrament: The Sacred Heart of Christ's Church is the Canonized Mass as instituted by

Christ (but not Bugnini); as canonized by the *sensus et praxis fidelium* and as specifically and "officially" canonized by the Council of Trent; and *Quo Primum* (for all subsequent time in the Latin Rite). During the Bishops' Revolt, this Sacred Heart of Catholicism has been taken away by malfeasant clergymen. In place of the living Sacred Heart, they have mandated counter-productive and sacrilegious communal celebration. They have replaced God with man. The Bishops and their "New Mass" have "made a difficulty where there should be no difficulty!"

The Bishops, posing as Catholic prelates, demand allegiance to an invalid, sacrilegious and apostate Mass-mocking service–the "New Mass." To do so, they often invoke papal authority.

Never Properly, Plainly, Plenarily or Papally Decreed

"I vow to change nothing of the received Tradition, and nothing thereof I have found before me guarded by my God-pleasing predecessors, to encroach upon, to alter, or to permit any innovation therein..."

Pope St. Agatho, (678-681) Papal Coronation Oath

The Bishops' Liturgical Revolution was orchestrated

under the non-pope-ing, benign leadership of the "Bishops of Rome" – Pope Paul VI and Pope John Paul II, who refused to pope plainly, properly or plenarily. Therefore, since "New Mass" has no binding or valid legal status on a par with the Canonized Latin Mass, the Pope's "will" in this matter is not only opposable, but must be opposed. Irrefutable, dogmatically binding Liturgical Church Law *(Lex Orandi)* cannot be replaced. If such were possible, a "plainly clear" and "more strongly binding (or dogmatic)" papal decree is needed. Such has not and cannot be done to sustain and impose the "New Mass." The authentic liturgical law of the "Latin land" (the Roman Patriarchate) is and will always be the Canonized Latin Mass.

Opposable Popes; "Deposable" Bishops

From the earliest times, the Church has insisted on allegiance to Christ through the full and exclusive acceptance of Apostolic Tradition. The *sensus et praxis fidelium* and dogmatic Church pronouncements have irrevocably pronounced the Canonized Latin Mass Rite to be dogmatically and irrevocably binding. *Quo Primum,* teaches that it is the grave duty of Bishops not to permit any other liturgy for the Latin Rite than the Canonized Latin Mass Text as spelled out in missals (printed before 1950). Bishops have failed God. They have sinned, *"maxima culpa."*

> **"We determine and order by this Our decree, to be valid in perpetuity, that never shall anything be added to, omitted from or changed in this Missal...."**
> ***Quo Primum,* Pope St. Pius V**

Rome has spoken! Thus, Christ has spoken! The Pope has made a dogmatic decree. *"Anathema sit"* anyone who disobeys! This, by itself, is the "preponderance of evidence" needed to conclude to the invalidity of "New Mass."

> **"It is certainly not the function of the Holy See to introduce Church reforms. It is the first duty of the pope to watch over and safeguard the traditions of the Church–her dogmatic, moral and liturgical traditions."**
> ***Liturgical Revolution,* Klaus Gamber, p. 38**

Evidently, Pope Paul VI certainly knew this. Realizing that he could not officially bind Catholics to accept any "New Mass" Liturgy as Catholic, he decided instead to merely attempt to add four such liturgical prayers to the Canon of the missal. Furthermore, he introduced the Novus Ordo with "wishful thinking words" that do not bind anyone. He said in the New Roman Missal:

> **"We hope that this missal will be received by the Faithful. We wish that these...prescriptions may be firm and effective."** **Pope Paul VI, April 3, 1969**

He wishes and hopes that all may accept these "canons" (sic) as additions (whatever that may mean). To clarify his non-authoritative decision, he later admitted:

> **"This rite (New Mass) and its related rubrics are not in themselves a dogmatic definition."**
> **Pope Paul VI, Nov. 19, 1969**

Clearly, the enigmatic Pope Paul VI himself never attempted to issue a "clearly and fully binding imposition" of the new rite because he realized that he could not overturn the dogma of the Church, binding since the time of Christ, re-iterated by the Council of Trent, *Quo Primum, Apostolicae Curae* and *Veterum Sapientia.* Effectively, local Bishops, not the modern popes, are the "Judases" of our day. Today, Peter betrayed Christ by not stopping Judas-Bishops from daily sacrileging the Most Holy. Either the Church is a fake; or, if it is not, then *Quo Primum* is still in effect and remains in effect *in perpetuity*; and, to say or attend a "New Mass" (as if it were a Mass) *ipso facto* constitutes apostasy.

Also, recall that Vatican Council Two was *pastoral (and not dogmatic,* as explicitly stated by both of the Council Popes). Furthermore, no one can credibly claim that the Bishops of Vatican Two "gave us" or "approved of" "New Mass." They could not because such a Mass-mocking liturgy was not celebrated at the Council; nor, was it proposed, studied or approved. Why, then, did Pope Paul VI, in effect, "green-light" such a Mass-mocking liturgy (knowing full well that it would replace the Canonized Latin Mass Liturgy)? Jean Guitton, the confidante of Pope Paul VI, assures us:

> **"The intention of Paul VI with regard to what is commonly called the Mass was to reform the Catholic liturgy in such a way that it should coincide with the Protestant liturgy. There was, with Paul VI, an ecumenical intention to remove, or, at least, to correct, or, at least, to relax, what was too Catholic in the traditional sense in the Mass and, I repeat, to get the Catholic Mass closer to the Calvinist Mass."**
>
> **Jean Guitton, as stated in *Latin Mass Magazine,* Winter 1995**

On this testimony of Jean Guitton, the "apostate nature" of the "New Mass" text is once again verified. By his "negligence in office," Pope Paul VI, insured that Catholics would be subjected to an apostate liturgy and, thereby, to a false religion. A "Protestant Mass" is an act of apostasy and is, in itself, invalid. It cannot be binding, nor can it be valid. Anglicans or "New Mass" alleged "Catholics,"who use a Mass-simulation in place of the Canonized Holy Mass, are apostates. One could contend that Pope Paul VI merely tolerated an experimentation with the new "mass-like" service. However, this "license to experiment," when inserted into the liberal Bishops' prevailing anti-Tridentine mind-set, insured that experimentation would soon metamorphosize into imposition and become the unlawful "law of the land."

As it were, washing his hands of all guilt, Pope Paul VI, when promulgating the "New Mass," clearly decreed that *"The rite ...by itself is not a dogmatic definition...*Pope Paul VI, 11/19/69." *De facto,* the Pope admitted that the whole "'New Mass' economy," not being a dogmatic definition, could not in any way replace the "dogmatic Canonized Latin Mass economy or dispensation." Christ's Canonized Latin Mass remains the only valid and legal Mass Rite for the Latin Rite, since it is such according to Catholic dogma, as even Pope Paul VI recognized (and by his deeds, in effect, violated).

One could argue that Pope Paul VI merely attempted to restrict and "reign in" the already existing legion of episcopally imposed eucharistic prayers–limiting them to four (as he specified). However, what good was *Missale Romanum* ? What was the result?

Within a year of its publication, the "New Mass" had multiplied from the "approved four" to well over two hundred more "similarly spirited" Mass simulations or eucharistic type prayers in use within the Latin Patriarchate. Such a restrictive plan failed miserably. Indeed, the name of "New Mass," even in our day, aptly remains "legion" (cf Mk 5:9).

> **"Those, therefore, who, after the manner of wicked heresies, dare to set aside ecclesiastical traditions; and to invent any kind of novelty; or, to reject any of those things entrusted to the Church; or, who wrongfully and outrageously devise the destruction of those traditions enshrined in the Catholic Church, are to be punished thus: if they are bishops, we order them to be deposed..."**
>
> **Second Council of Nicaea, 787**

Whether he realized it or not, from the revolting 1960's onward, each Pope, Bishop and Priest was given the fundamental liturgical option: be faithful to Christ and His liturgical Will or fail to be faithful.

> **"I myself was one of those who initially sinned in this regard. However, by God's special graces and my graced cooperation, I saw the truth and was graced to repentance. I now function as I was ordained (by "Holy Orders") to function–"to celebrate the Holy Sacrifice of the Mass for the living and the dead."**
>
> **Fr. Paul Trinchard**

Historically speaking, the "liturgical buck" is episcopal in origin and sustenance. However, this "buck" primarily confronts each person, especially, each Catholic priest (or, worse yet, each "non-Holy Ordered" "fake priest." How will he decide?

The Origin of the Bishops' Liturgical Buck

> **"It was in that year, 1962, that a schismatic heretical, Conciliar sect of the Church in the United States was born...the majority of our American bishops refused to obey. I should know because I was there...at the time."**
> Fr. Gommar de Pauw, *Conciliar or Catholic, 1967,* Prof. of Theology & Canon Law, www.traditio.com/tradlib/ depauw67.txt.p.9

According to history, the "New Mass" was "the Bishops' dastardly deed" (from the 1960's, continuing into the present). "Catholics" continue to be "spiritually raped" by their Bishops. Bishops force them into liturgical apostasy.

They must attend "New Masses" by episcopal decree or be declared schismatic. This "liturgical buck" starts, is reinforced and winds up at the Bishops' desks. Sacrilegious, unlawful "New Mass" texts continue to be imposed as substitutes for the Canonized Latin Mass Text by individual Bishops in their individual dioceses day by day.

> **"What you are attending today in the churches of our once Catholic Church establishment–what you are witnessing is no longer a valid Sacrifice of the Mass."**
> Fr. Gommar de Pauw, Professor of Theology & Doctor of Canon Law, *Conciliar or Catholic* Chicago IL 1967, www.traditio.com/tradlib/depauw67.txt, p.12

Concerning the Addition of St. Joseph to the Canon of Mass

WHAT SPIRIT INFORMS CHANGE?

Venerable Pope Pius IX (1846-1878

In response to requests that he add the name of St. Joseph to the Canon of the Mass, Venerable Pope Pius IX stated:

> **"I am only the pope. What power have I to touch the Canon?"**
> **www.traditio.com, *The Limitations of Papal Authority*, p. 10**

POPE LEO XIII (1878-1903)

Pope Leo XIII, who had named St. Joseph as the Patron of the Universal Church and had written an encyclical letter about him, refused permission for the addition of the saint's name to the Canon of the Mass, citing the tradition of the Church that the Canon was to remain unchanged.
www.traditio.com, *The Limitations of Papal Authority,* p. 12

POPES ST. GREGORY I, THE GREAT (590-604)

The Mass as said by Pope St. Gregory is the same Canonized Latin Mass of today. The Mass was affirmed to be complete and unchangeable since Apostolic Times. Since that time, no pope has dared to change the Ordo of the Traditional Latin Mass, until in 1962, Pope John XXIII added "beati Joseph, eiusdem Virginis Sponsi" [of blessed Joseph, Spouse of the same Virgin] to the Communicantes of the Canon.
www.traditio.com, *The Limitations of Papal Authority,* p. 1

JOHN XXIII (1958-1963)

Comment: Was not Pope John XXIII "testing the Spirit?" Why did he want to add St. Joseph when previous popes specifically refused such an addition?

"De Fide"

CHRIST INSTITUTED THE MASS

The essential elements of the Mass Liturgy do not and cannot *evolve.* These elements are "of faith" *(de fide)* since Christ instituted the Mass and Sacraments. The Canonized Latin Mass Text is "of Christ" not from men.

To be a Catholic, one must reverence and firmly believe in the Deposit of Faith (which includes liturgical morals). This "Deposit" was forever sealed at the death of the last Apostle.

Salutary belief is firm conviction which is given by God Hb 11:1. **Either one is convinced or not.**

The essential element characterizing and giving life to the Deposit of Faith is the Christ-given Mass Text which Christ and His Church demand that Holy Ordered priests use in order to "effect" Christ's Sacrifice and Christ's Sacrament, alive in our midst. Christ instituted the Canonized Latin Mass Text (the Ordinary Canon from *Suscipe Sancte Pater...*to...*Per Ipsum).*

This fact cannot be historically disproved. It is an essential element of the Catholic Faith. To deny this is to become an apostate.

Chapter Eleven

CARDINAL OTTAVIANI EVALUATES THE "NEW MASS"

These high ranking prelates, including the Prefect of the Faith, Cardinal Ottaviani, prove that "New Mass" is invalid, according to the preponderance of evidence.

Sufficient evidence against the validity of the "New Mass" was given by none other than Alfredo Cardinal Ottaviani, who, at the time of the formulation of the "New Mass" sacrilege, was the head theologian of the Church, the Prefect of the Faith. He, along with Cardinal Bacci and others, evaluated the Novus Ordo standard (which was ultra conservative in comparison to its ever-changing degenerate progeny now in existence in parishes in the United States and elsewhere).

This "official evaluation" is called *THE OTTAVIANI INTERVENTION: Critical Study of the Novus Ordo Liturgy* (9/25/1969). Significant critical words within this document are quoted and appear italicized below.

The Novus Ordo Liturgy:

- *"as a whole and in its parts departs from the Catholic Faith."*
  [It is anti-Catholic.]

- *"satisfies the most modernist of Protestants."*
  [Ecumenically, it is evil.]

- *"the celebrant appears to be nothing more than a protestant minister."*
  [In itself, it rejects the Catholic priesthood.]

- *"The people never asked for this."* [It] *"was launched as pluralistic and experimental...was rejected by the Synod of Bishops, was never submitted to the collegial judgment of the Episcopal Conference; the people, least of all in mission lands, never asked for any reform of Holy Mass whatsoever...one fails to comprehend the motives behind* [it]*...."*
  [It was imposed by apostate bishops.]

- [It is] *"... an incalculable error."*

- [It] *"...rejects the Real Presence, the reality of* [Christ's] *Sacrifice and the function of the consecrating priest."*

- **[It]** ***"is opposed to the religious spirit of the oriental Liturgies."***

- **[It replaces]** ***"divine sacrifice with human sacrifice."***
  [It is the liturgy of the Second Beast of the Apocalypse.]

- **[It]** ***"brings God bread and God turns it into bread of life...brings God wine and God turns it into spiritual drink."***

Comments on the Ottaviani Intervention

In effect, after studying the "New Mass," reminiscent of the "composers" of *Apostolicae Curae,* the Prefect of the Faith and his fellow theologian Cardinals concluded that the "New Mass" had to be invalid because of its religion or because of its "native character and spirit." The "New Mass" Novus Ordo Liturgy ***"as a whole and in its parts, departs from the Catholic Faith."***

It is ecumenically evil. It is so evil that the "New Mass" Liturgy cannot satisfy even fundamentalist Protestants, since it fails to give sufficient emphasis to; and, in effect, rejects, Catholic fiducial basics such as: sin,

Hell, damnation; and, Christ as Saviour. The "New Mass" Liturgy, indeed, ***"satisfies the most modernist of Protestants,"*** the worst heretics.

In fact, ***"the celebrant*** [in truth, the presider or facilitator] ***appears to be nothing more than a protestant minister."*** Therefore, (Mass-wise) one must conclude from applying *Apostolicae Curae* that: the Bishops' "New Ordinal," as well as, Service are *'null, void and sacrilegious... --Pope Leo XIII."* They are "conclusively invalid and sacrilegious."

Why was the "New Mass" fabricated? ***"The people never asked for this."*** This "New Mass" Rite ***"was launched as pluralistic and experimental...was rejected by the Synod of Bishops, was never submitted to the collegial judgment of the Episcopal Conference... the people, least of all in mission lands never asked for any reform of Holy Mass whatsoever...one fails to comprehend the motives behind...*** **[it]*."***

Cardinal Ottaviani could not bring himself to explicitly confess that this was the liturgy of anti-Christ, the Abominable Desolation, the unholy in the place of the Most Holy. He did confess that the Novus Ordo "New Mass" Liturgy was ***"an incalculable error,"*** the worst mistake the existential church has ever made in allowing this experiment.

Because of this "incalculable error" the post-Vatican Two establishment constitutes the worst church under the worst popes (Popes Paul VI and John Paul II) in the history of Catholicism. Its episcopally imposed "New Mass" is anti-Christ and anti-Church.

The New Service ***"rejects the Real Presence, the reality of* [Christ's] *Sacrifice and the function of the consecrating priest."*** Even though claiming to have borrowed a wealth of piety from the Eastern Churches, the "New Mass" Liturgy mocks the Mass and ***"is opposed to the religious spirit of the oriental Liturgies."***

The "New Mass" Liturgy replaces ***"divine sacrifice with human sacrifice."*** It is far worse than the dogmatically condemned Anglican Liturgy. The latter offers "our bounden duty to God." The Bishops' "New Mass" ***"brings God bread and God turns it into bread of life...brings God wine and God turns it into spiritual drink."*** The Anglican Liturgy has man serve God. The Bishops' "New Mass," in gross sacrilege, has God serve man!

How did Pope Paul VI take this attack against him made by the "official intervention" on September 25, 1969? A "silly," sarcastic and juvenile response was given by Pope Paul VI on November 19, 1969. "Tongue in cheek," he claims that the Church of Vatican Two demanded that he simplify the Mass Rites. Sarcastically, and in Mad Hatter fashion, he stated:

> **"The Mass of the new rite is and remains the same Mass we have always had. If anything, its sameness has been brought out more clearly...,"**
> **Pope Paul VI, Nov. 19, 1969**

Equivalently, Pope Paul says that Joe is so much like his brother that he is more like his brother than his brother is like unto himself. The Mad Hatter strikes again!

Jesus once asked the rhetorical question: "What father will give his child a stone to eat or a poisonous serpent to clutch?" Now, this question has been expunged from the rhetorical list. Now we know, since we are victimized by ecclesial fathers who do the "incomprehensively evil!"

Eventually Evil Bleeds Through

> **"A person who has correctly and seriously used the requisite matter and form to effect and confer a sacrament is presumed for that very reason to have intended to do (interdisse) what the Church does."** Pope Leo XIII, *Apostolicae Curae, On the Nullity of Anglican Orders,* 1896

A "good-intentioned" and "sufficiently conscious or aware" Holy Ordered priest (one ordained before 1969 or so) cannot say a valid Mass using the invalid form or formulation of "New Mass." (Pope Leo XIII *Apostolicae Curae.)* **This principle was dogmatically employed by Pope Leo XIII to condemn Anglican services and ordinals: in the "last analysis," the "sacramental or Mass intent" and, thereby, the validity must be judged by the words used, omitted or modified (relative to the norm) within these texts (ordinals or services).**

Here, one can understand why the Church defines a proper sacrament in terms of proper as "Church-defined" words. The crucial intent (e.g. to obey Christ or not to do so) flows from conformity to Christ-given canonized words. For example, one cannot confer a valid Baptism saying,"I baptize you into the community of Christ" (no matter what the intent).

Cardinal Ottaviani, the head theologian of his times and his high-ranking prelates, in studying the "holiest worded" New Order Mass-like extant set of prayers, concluded, in effect, that its matter "led to" or "made for" invalidity. No Mass could possibly result from consciously using any of the sets of Mass-mocking words as are found in the New Order Services, (including the rarely used Eucharistic Prayer One, since this prayer or "alleged Mass text" does not conform to the Canonized Latin Mass Text).

Chapter Twelve

LEONINE PRINCIPLES PROVE "NEW MASS" INVALID

The proper application of the following Leonine Principles provides preponderance of evidence to conclude to the invalidity of "New Mass."

---

1) Apostolic Tradition: Liturgy must be from Christ. If a liturgy is new; alien to the Faith; an aberration from the body of truth of the Catholic Church; does not originate from Christ through Apostolic Tradition; then, it cannot be Catholic and it is invalid.

Briefly stated, Leonine Principles are the dogmatic facts and the thinking already established through the centuries by the Church as binding. These principles were expounded by the commission appointed by Pope Leo XIII to dogmatically and irreversibly underline by decree that Anglican Ordination and Services are invalid. This final determination is set forth in Pope Leo's *Apostolicae Curae,* written in 1896.

Various Leonine Principles are considered. If a purported Mass liturgy is not from Christ; or, if it is

a significant aberration from the body of truth that is the Catholic Church; if it is new and alien to the Faith; or, if it is not to be found in Apostolic Tradition; or, it expresses and prays heresy; then, it cannot be Catholic; it is not valid. Pope Leo XIII used this Church-proclaimed, dogmatic criteria to determine that the Anglican "New Mass" Liturgy and Ordinals are not valid. Pope Leo XIII used Christ-given Church criteria to properly pope!

---

2) The "mininal words approach" to validity is acceptable only within an orthodox context. The "eight magic words" or even the "twenty-two essential consecration words" must exist within the Canonized Mass and not merely as Mass simulation, which, of its very nature, does not "essentially agree with" but "essentially is at odds with" the Catholic religion of and in Christ's Canonized Latin Mass Liturgy.

In effect, *Apostolicae Curae* assured us that the "minimal words approach" was acceptable only within an orthodox context. The very nature of the Anglican Liturgy did not "essentially agree with," but was "essentially at odds with" the Catholic Liturgy and religion. Neither the Anglican "New Mass" nor the Bishops' "New Mass" intends to have a Holy Ordered priest celebrate the Holy Sacrifice of the Mass as instituted by Christ and canonized by His Church.

"The New Liturgy was as little a translation of the Latin Missal as similar Lutheran Missals which are based upon the design of getting rid of the sacrificial character of the Mass altogether...The contemptuous and wholesale destruction of the ancient altars and the substitution of tables is sufficient to show that the abolition of the Holy Sacrifice was envisioned by the Anglicans."

The Abbot & Me On Liturgy, Fr. Paul Trinchard, from Cardinal Gasquet's *Advent Sermons*, 1913

---

3) **If the rite is changed with the intention of introducing a new rite and rejecting what the institution of Christ does; what belongs to the nature of the sacrament; then it is clear that the intention is adverse to and destructive of the Sacrament, rendering it invalid.**

4) **Being cognizant of the necessary connection between faith and worship, if the animus of the authors is contrary to the Catholic Church, even under pretext of returning to primitive forms, it is a corruption of the liturgy, so as to conform to error. The "native character and spirit" or religion of "New Mass" renders it invalid.**

The address of Pope Paul VI of November 19, 1967, presents a clear application of No. 3: *"If the rite is changed with the intention of introducing a new rite...it is invalid." Lex credendi, lex orandi.*

Illicit liturgies produce schismatic churches. Invalid

liturgies produce apostate churches (protestant or "new age"). Is one not led to conclude that Catholics now abide in liturgical apostasy within, since the Bishops' "New Mass" is invalid?

"New Mass" contains, expresses and prays, not only heretically protestant, but, also, new age (or Novus Ordo Saeclorum) religions. Do not the observations of Abbot Gasquet (one of the principle composers of *Apostolicae Curae* for Pope Leo XIII and the Church) about the invalidity of the Anglican Liturgy apply, *a fortiori,* to the Bishops' "New Mass?"

Both honest authorities and those endowed with a religious sense have no problem perceiving that the Bishops' "New Mass" embodies and expresses a false religion. Some are even known to say: *"It's a whole new religion–and I like it!"* (Any religion other than the *semper ubique idem* religion of the Catholic Church is a false and damning religion). It is not orthodox. Others remark as follows:

> **"The real destruction of the traditional Mass, of the traditional Roman Rite is the wholesale destruction of the faith on which it was based."**
> ***Christian Order,* quote by Msgr. Klaus Gamber, March 1994, p. 188**

"The role of the priest is falsified. The priest is now a mere president or brother, rather than the consecrated minister who celebrates Mass 'in the person of Christ...' It is obvious that the New Order of Mass has no intention of presenting the Faith to which the Catholic conscience is bound forever."
Ottaviani Intervention, **Sections V, VI**

---

5) The New Services (Anglican and *a fortiori* Novus Ordo) are invalid since "New Masses" emanate from, express and fortify a new, anti-Church, anti-Christ religion.

"If the rite be changed with the intention of introducing a new rite and rejecting what the institution of [or by] Christ does and what belongs to the nature of the sacrament....then it is clear that the intention or design is adverse to and destructive of the Sacrament [i.e. renders it invalid]**.....**

The animus of the authors was contrary to or opposed to the Catholic Church....Being cognizant of the necessary connection between faith and worship... under pretext of returning to primitive forms, they corrupted liturgy so as to conform it to their errors."
Apostolicae Curae, **#30, 1896**

Apostolicae Curae **of 1896, dogmatically pronounced Anglican Orders to be invalid. Pope Leo XIII singled out one factor as vital; on it, his central argument depends. It is the 'native character and spirit' [or religion] of the Ordinal [as well as, of the Service or "Mass"].** ***Eucharistic Sacrifice and the Reformation,*** **Francis Clark, S.J., Oxford, 1967, p. 16**

Just as the "native character and spirit" of Anglican Orders and Services determined their invalidity, so also do the "native character and spirit" of the Bishops' "New Mass" Service and their post-1969 "New Ordinal" determine their invalidity. A word for word comparison (as demonstrated elsewhere in this book) of the Offertory and Consecration prayers within Christ's Canonized Latin Mass, the Anglican Service and the Bishops' "New Mass" will lead one to conclude that, since the Anglican Service is held to be invalid, *a fortiori,* the "New Mass," being a further departure from the Catholic Mass than the Anglican "New Mass," logically, must also be invalid. [See *Abbot & Me On Liturgy,* available from MAETA, for Abbot Gasquet's comparison of the Catholic Mass with the Anglican and for Fr. Trinchard's comparison of the Catholic Mass, the Anglican Service and the Novus Ordo Liturgy. Also, to be graced with a truly Catholic knowledge of, appreciation for; and, dedication to the Canonized Latin Mass, read *Latin Mass Prayers Explained.]*

In God's order, policemen, even Roman police, need be feared only by criminals. In the Novus Ordo (New Age), policemen will exterminate authentic Catholics who believe in God and His absolute Truth; and profess Christ's Canonized Mass Liturgy as being the one and only Canonized Mass Liturgy of the Latin Rite. Indeed, "they' have begun quite successfully.

> **"Nothing is more dangerous than the heretics who...corrupt with a single word, like a drop of poison, the purity and simplicity of the faith which we have received through tradition from God and through the Apostles." --Pope Leo XIII**

Catholic Mass versus the "New Mass" (Anglican)

"In brief, it is impossible for any unbiased mind to compare the ancient Canon of the Holy Mass with the New Liturgy, without seeing that both in spirit and substance it was conceived [like the Bishops' "New Mass"] **with the desire of getting rid of the Catholic Mass altogether.**

Today we find men of intelligence and good faith claiming to have the same Christ-given sacrifice and the same sacrificing priests as the Catholic Church, while they are using a new man-made liturgy from which, of set purpose, every notion of Oblation and Sacrifice has been ruthlessly removed...To anyone who will put the one [liturgy] **by the side of the other and note the changes and omissions, it must appear as clear as the noonday sun that there is an essential and substantial doctrinal difference between the two liturgies.**

Radical religious changes were made. They reflect and teach an essential denial of Catholic Dogma.

Aidan Cardinal Gasquet, *Sermons in Advent,* 1913, St. Patrick's Cathedral, N.Y., brackets added. It was Cardinal Gasquet whose commission wrote the *de fide* condemnation of the Anglican "New Mass."

On the Validity of Holy Orders

Within this book which primarily address the invalidity of "New Mass," is is also necessary to dwell on the "fake orders" received within the Novus Ordo. Already, as of this initial writing, signs exists pointing to the establishment controlled "reinstatement" of the right of a priest to say the "Latin Mass."

Two problems will arise:

Will the Mass be the Canonized Latin Mass Rite Text?

Will alleged priests and bishops be validly ordained Holy Ordered Priests?

One must recall Pope Leo XIII's *Apostolicae Curae* --On the Nullity of Anglican Orders–(which today's church never applies to its Anglican or Episcopalian converts). *Apostolicae Curae,* when applied to "'priests' ordained after 1970 by the rite of that time" assures us that they are still laymen. Laymen cannot celebrate Mass.

> **If anyone saith...that those who have neither been rightly ordained, nor sent, by ecclesiastical and canonical power, but come from elsewhere, are lawful ministers of the word and of the sacraments; let him be anathema.**
>
> Council of Trent, Sess. XXIII, Can. 7, D. 967

Chapter Thirteen

APOSTOLICAE CURAE RELEVANT YESTERDAY TODAY & FOREVER

Pope Leo XIII's *Apostolicae Curae* constitutes the basis of argumentation proving that "New Mass" is conclusively invalid. *Apostolicae Curae* provides "Leonine Principles." It applies these principles to Anglican Ordinals and Services. Applying these principles in like manner to the Bishops' "New Mass" and "New Ordinal" one is led to conclude that the Bishops' "New Mass" and "New Ordinal" are, indeed, invalid. *Apostolicae Curae,* applied to "priests ordained after 1970 by the rite of that time," assures one that they are still laymen. Laymen cannot celebrate Mass. The establishment now indicates a "controlled reinstatement" of the right of a priest to say "Latin-worded Mass." Since the validity of "services is determined by the validity of ordinals and vice versa," two problems will arise:

Will the Mass be the Canonized Latin Rite Mass Text?

Will alleged priests and bishops be validly ordained Holy Ordered Priests?

"In brief, it is impossible for any unbiased mind to compare the ancient Canon of the Holy Mass with the New Liturgy without seeing that both in spirit and substance [like unto the Bishops' "New Mass"] **it was conceived with the desire of getting rid of the Catholic Mass altogether. Today we find men of intelligence and good faith claiming to have the same Christ-given sacrifice and the same sacrificing priests as the Catholic Church, while they are using a new man-made liturgy from which, of set purpose, every notion of Oblation and Sacrifice has been ruthlessly removed...**

To anyone who will put the one [liturgy] **by the side of the other and note the changes and omissions, it must appear as clear as the noonday sun that there is an essential and substantial doctrinal difference between the two liturgies.**

Radical religious changes were made. They reflect and teach an essential denial of Catholic Dogma."

Aidan Cardinal Gasquet, *Sermons in Advent,* 1913, St. Patrick's Cathedral, N.Y.,Card. Gasquet headed the commission writing the *de fide* condemnation of the Anglican "New Mass," *Apostolicae Curae.* Brackets added.

Text and Comment
On the Nullity of Anglican Orders

1. **We have dedicated to the welfare of the noble English nation no small portion of the Apostolic care and charity by which, helped by His grace, we endeavor to fulfil the office and follow in the footsteps of "the Great Pastor of the sheep," Our Lord Jesus Christ. The letter which last year we sent to the English seeking the Kingdom of Christ in the unity of the faith is a special witness of our good will towards England. In it we recalled the memory of the ancient union of the people with Mother Church, and we strove to hasten the day of a happy reconciliation by stirring up men's hearts to offer diligent prayer to God. And, again, more recently, when it seemed good to Us to treat more fully the unity of the Church in a General Letter...in the hope that our teaching might both strengthen Catholics and provide the saving light to those divided from us. It is pleasing to acknowledge the generous way in which our zeal and plainness of speech, inspired by no mere human motives, have met the approval of the English people, and this testifies not less to their courtesy than to the solicitude of many for their eternal salvation.**

2. **With the same mind and intention, we have now determined to turn our consideration to a matter of no less importance, which is closely connected with the same subject and with our holy desires.**

Comment:

The Anglican "bishops" are not priests. They are

laymen. The Catholic view contrasts with this Anglican "New Ordinal" position. Pope Leo XIII wished to convert these Anglican heretics. Unlike "post-Vatican II" Popes, he refused to convey any impression that he recognized them as being "other than apostates." They were (and still are) fake priests and bishops who say invalid Mass-mocking services.

3. **For an opinion already prevalent, confirmed more than once by the action and constant practice of the Church, maintained that when in England, shortly after it was rent from the center of Christian Unity, a new rite for conferring Holy Orders was publicly introduced under Edward VI. The true Sacrament of Order as instituted by Christ lapsed, and with it the hierarchical succession. For some time, however, and in these last years especially, a controversy has sprung up as to whether the Sacred Orders conferred according to the Edwardine Ordinal possessed the nature and effect of a Sacrament, those in favor of the absolute validity, or of a doubtful validity, being not only certain Anglican writers, but some few Catholics, chiefly non-English. The consideration of the excellency of the Christian priesthood moved Anglican writers in this matter, desirous as they were that their own people should not lack the twofold power over the Body of Christ, Catholic writers were impelled by a wish to smooth the way for the return of Anglicans to holy unity. Both, indeed, thought that in view of studies brought up to the level of recent research, and of new documents rescued from oblivion, it was not inopportune to reexamine the question by our authority.**

Comment:
We work and pray that papal authority will be led by God to examine the "New Mass," as well as, all other fundamental characteristics of the Bishops' newly imposed "religion.". To bring this about, we hope, at the very least, to raise the question of the invalidity of the "New Mass" and "New Ordinal" to the level of "worthy controversy," controversy of infinite importance.

4. **And we, not disregarding such desires and opinions, above all, obeying the dictates of apostolic charity, have considered that nothing should be left untried that might in any way tend to preserve souls from injury or procure their advantage. It has, therefore, pleased Us to graciously permit the cause to be reexamined, so that, through the extreme care taken in the new examination, all doubt, or even shadow of doubt, should be removed for the future.**

5. **To this end we commissioned a certain number of men noted for their learning and ability, whose opinions in this matter were known to be divergent, to state the grounds of their judgment in writing. We then, having summoned them to our person, directed them to interchange writings and furthe to investigate and discuss all that was necessary for a full knowledge of the matter. We were careful, also, that they should be able to reexamine all documents bearing on this question which were known to exist in the Vatican archives, to search for new ones, and even have at their disposal all acts relating to this subject which are preserved by the Holy Office as it is called, the Supreme Council and to consider whatever had up to this time been adduced by learned men on both sides. We ordered them,**

when prepared in this way, to meet together in special sessions. These, to the number of twelve, were held under the presidency of one of the Cardinals of the Holy Roman Church, appointed by ourself, and all were invited to free discussion. Finally, we directed that the acts of these meetings, together with all other documents, should be submitted to our venerable brethren, the Cardinals of the same Council, so that when all had studied the whole subject, and discussed it in our presence, each might give his own opinion.

Comment:
As it were, we here witness *"fides quarens intellectum"* in action. The issue was already settled by the Holy See: Anglican Services and Ordinals were invalid or null and void. However, to help individuals to remove any doubts or hesitancy, a thorough exam was papally decreed.

9. **To all rightly estimating these matters it will not be difficult to understand why, in the Letters of Julius...issued to the Apostolic Legate on 8 March 1554, there is a distinct mention, first of those, who, "rightly and lawfully promoted," might be maintained in their orders: and then of others "not promoted to Holy Orders" might "be promoted if they were found to be worthy and fitting subjects." For it is clearly and definitely noted, as indeed was the case, that there were two classes of men; the first of those who had really received Holy Orders, either before the secession of Henry VIII, or, if after it, and by ministers infected by error and schism, still according to the accustomed Catholic rite; the second, those who were initiated according to the Edwardine Ordinal, who on that**

account could not be "promoted," since they had received an ordination which was null.

Comment:
Note in #9 that the criteria for determining the validity of Holy Orders is the use of the Catholic Ordinal. Replacing the Catholic Ordinal with another one, in itself, indicates and issues from a will to invalidate Holy Orders, a will (as in the Bishops' "New Ordinal") to commission presiders, facilitators or ministers–a determination to totally reject and deny the conferral of Holy Orders. Such was the case with the Anglicans. Such is the case now with the Bishops' "New Mass" and "New Ordinals." Also, one may profitably note that invalidity is determined by the refusal to use the Catholic Rite.

22. **It must be clear to everyone that the controversy lately revived had already been definitely settled by the Apostolic See, and that it is to the insufficient knowledge of these documents that we must, perhaps, attribute the fact that any Catholic writer should have considered it still an open question.**

23. **But, as we stated at the beginning, there is nothing we so deeply and ardently desire as to be of help to men of good will by showing them the greatest consideration and charity. Wherefore, we ordered that the Anglican Ordinal, which is the essential point of the whole matter, should be once more most carefully examined.**

24. **In the examination of any rite for the effecting and administering of Sacraments, distinction is rightly made between the part which is ceremonial and that which is essential, the latter being usually called the "matter and form." All know that the Sacraments of the New Law, as sensible and efficient signs of invisible grace, ought both to signify the grace which they effect, and effect the grace which they signify. Although the signification ought to be found in the whole essential rite, that is to say, in the "matter and form," it still pertains chiefly to the "form;" since the "matter" is the part which is not determined by itself, but which is determined by the "form." And this appears still more clearly in the Sacrament of Order, the "matter" of which, in so far as we have to consider it in this case, is the imposition of hands, which, indeed, by itself signifies nothing definite, and is equally used for several Orders and for Confirmation.**

Comment:
Rome has spoken; the issue is settled. Theologians of adequate knowledge and minimal good will should have been able to see that Rome had spoken concerning the Anglican Ordinal and Service well before *Apostolicae Curae* was written. So, too, *before* an *Apostolicae Curae* is written for the Bishops' "New Mass," one should be already convinced of the invalidity of the Bishops' "New Ordinal" and "New Service." Like *Apostolicae Curae,* this book is written to help men of good will to perceive the ugly truth about the Bishops' "New Ordinal" and "New Mass."

25. **But the words which until recently were commonly held by Anglicans to constitute the proper form of priestly ordination, namely, "Receive the Holy Ghost," certainly do not in the least definitely express the sacred Order of Priesthood (sacerdotium) or its grace and power, which chiefly the power "of consecrating and of offering the true Body and Blood of the Lord" (Council of Trent, Sess. XXIII, de Sacr. Ord., Canon 1) in that sacrifice which is no "bare commemoration of the sacrifice offered on the Cross" (Ibid. Sess XXII., de Sacrif. Missae, Canon 3).**

Comment:
The argumentation for the invalidity of the "New Mass" and "New Ordinal" is based on number "25." For example, not even the presence of 8, or even 22 minimal words of Consecration–as exists in Anglican New Mass–would render the Bishops' "New Mass" valid. Why? Saying Mass and "Holy Ordering" are religious acts which are to be done as Christ instituted them to be done; as His Church decrees; and, as the the *sensus et praxis fidelium* has spelled out since Apostolic Times.

The Anglican has 22 minimal words. Their "New Mass" is dogmatically invalid. The Bishops' "New Mass" lacks/distorts even these words. On this count alone, the Bishops' "New Mass" is invalid. However, even were the Bishops to imitate the Anglican and use these minimal words, the religion or "native character and spirit" of the Bishops' "New Mass" would render them "all the more likely invalid" than the Anglican Services.

26. **This form had, indeed, afterwards added to it the words "for the office and work of a priest," etc.; but this rather shows that the Anglicans themselves perceived that the first form was defective and inadequate. But even if this addition could give to the form its due signification, it was introduced too late, as a century had already elapsed since the adoption of the Edwardian Ordinal, for, as the Hierarchy had become extinct, there remained no power of ordaining.**

Comment:
In 1970, the Bishops' Ordination Rite was radically changed. According to Pope Leo's *Apostolicae Curae,* thereby the Bishops' "New Ordinal" lost the power of ordaining.

27. **In vain has help been recently sought for the plea of the validity of Anglican Orders from the other prayers of the same Ordinal. For, to put aside other reasons which show this to be insufficient for the purpose in the Anglican life, let this argument suffice for all. From them have been deliberately removed whatever sets forth the dignity and office of the priesthood in the Catholic rite. That "form" consequently cannot be considered apt or sufficient for the Sacrament which omits what it ought essentially to signify.**

28. **The same holds good of episcopal consecration. For to the formula, "Receive the Holy Ghost," not only were the words "for the office and work of a bishop," etc. added at a later period, but even these, as we shall presently state, must be understood in a sense different to that which bear in the Catholic rite. Nor is anything gained by quoting the**

prayer of the preface, "Almighty God," since it, in like manner, has been stripped of the words which denote the *summon sacerdotium.*

Comment:
"From them [Ordinals specifically; and, Services, implicitly] have been deliberately removed whatever sets forth the dignity and office of the priesthood [and, for the Bishop's "New Mass"] in the Catholic rite...." Several chapters in this book use this principle and illustrate its application to "New Mass" (and "New Ordinal"). The invalidity of "New Mass" (and, especially, "New Ordinal") is conclusively proven to be true from Pope Leo's words ("what has been deliberately removed #27"). As stated elsewhere, the Canonized Latin Mass Text is *the standard of judgment.* Significant deviation from this Text invalidates the "Mass mockery" which was thereby created. Such, in effect, is the criteria given by the Catholic Church through its dogmatic condemnations of Anglican "New Mass."

Positively stated, *Apostolicae Curae* dogmatizes that ordination rites, to be authentic or effective "must be understood in the same sense as the Catholic rite." To assure that this applies, one must use the (classical extant) Catholic Rite and nothing else. To use "something else" *ipso facto* sacrileges the bastardization. This is clear for Baptism. To say "I baptize you into Christ" renders the sacrament sacrileged and invalid.

29. **It is not relevant to examine here whether the episcopate be a completion of the priesthood or an order distinct from it; or whether, when bestowed, as they say *per saltum,* on one who is not a priest, it has or has not its effect. But the episcopate undoubtedly, by the institution of Christ, most truly belongs to the Sacrament of Order and constitutes the *sacerdotium* in the highest degree, namely, that which by the teaching of the Holy Fathers and our liturgical customs is called the *Summum sacerdotium sacri ministerii summa.* So it comes to pass that, as the Sacrament of Order and the true *sacerdotium* of Christ were utterly eliminated from the Anglican rite, and hence the *sacerdotium* is in no wise conferred truly and validly in the episcopal consecration of the same rite, for the like reason, therefore, the episcopate can in no wise be licitly and validly conferred by it, and this the more so because among the first duties of the episcopacy is that of ordaining ministers for the Holy Eucharist and sacrifice.**

Comment:

The Bishops' "New Ordinal" alleged "priests" are purposely *not ordained to celebrate the Holy Sacrifice of the Mass* (and, thereby, cannot bring Holy Sacrifice and Holy Sacrament into "here and now" mystical/sacramental existence). Period. Likewise, the Bishops' "New Masses" are purposely *"not designed nor created to be"* Holy Sacrifices of the Mass (as defined by binding Catholic theology). Therefore, "New Masses" are invalid. Period.

30. **For the full and accurate understanding of the Anglican Ordinal, besides what we have noted as to some of its parts, there is nothing more pertinent than to consider carefully the circumstances under which it was composed and publicly authorized. It would be tedious to enter into details, nor is it necessary to do so, as the history of that time is sufficiently eloquent as to the animus of the authors of the Ordinal against the Catholic Church; as to the abettors whom they associated with themselves from the heterodox sects; and as to the end they had in view. Being fully cognizant of the necessary connection between faith and worship, between 'the law of believing and the law of praying,' under a pretext of returning to the primitive form, they corrupted the Liturgical Order in many ways to suit the errors of the reformers. For this reason, in the whole Ordinal, not only is there no clear mention of the sacrifice, of consecration, of the priesthood *(sacerdotium)* and of the power of consecrating and offering sacrifice but, as we have just stated, every trace of these things which had been in such prayers of the Catholic rite as they had not entirely rejected, was deliberately removed and struck out.**

Comment:
Again, the previous comment applies to No. 30. *A fortiori,* Pope Leo's reasoning applies to the Bishops' "New Mass." Their "New Mass" is invalid. This book has proven such to be the case in the light of the religion or "theory of causality" employed by Pope Leo XIII to render a dogmatic judgment of invalidity.

31. **In this way, the native character or spirit, as it is called, of the Ordinal clearly manifests itself. Hence, if, vitiated in its origin, it was wholly insufficient, since no change had taken place. In vain those who, from the time of Charles I, have attempted to hold some kind of sacrifice or of priesthood, have made additions to the Ordinal. In vain, also, has been the contention of that small section of the Anglican body formed in recent times that the said Ordinal can be understood and interpreted in a sound and orthodox sense. Such efforts, we affirm, have been, and are, made in vain, and for this reason, that any words in the Anglican Ordinal, as it now is, which lend themselves to ambiguity, cannot be taken in the same sense as they possess in the Catholic rite. For once a rite has been initiated in which, as we have seen, the Sacrament of Order is adulterated or denied, and from which all idea of consecration and sacrifice has been rejected, the formula, "Receive the Holy Ghost" no longer holds good, because the Spirit is infused into the soul with the grace of the Sacrament, and so the words "for the office and work of a priest or bishop," and the like no longer holds good, but remain as words without the reality which Christ instituted.**

Comment:

The three previously cited paragraphs of the dogmatic *Apostolicae Curae* can be used to conclusively refute any major defense regarding the validity of the Bishops' "New Mass" for the very same reasons that Pope Leo XIII used to deny the validity of the Anglican "New Mass." The claim that "New Mass" contains the word "sacrifice" and, therefore, produces valid Holy Sacrifice of the Mass is in vain.

Catholic theology defines Holy Sacrifice of the Mass in a special and unique way. It is not a sacrifice (as in Anglican "New Mass": "the sacrifice of our bounden duty"). The Bishops' "New Mass" does not contain even this notion of sacrifice. Rather, "the people" say "New Mass," calling to mind and, thereby, allegedly "making present" Christ's passion, resurrection and ascension. "Sacrifice" or "oblation" (in the religion of the Bishops' "New Mass") is "through this very memorial" (paragraph 55 of Novus Ordo's *Institutio Generalis)*.

Catholicism believes in "the mystical/sacramental Holy Sacrifice of the Mass as celebrated by a Holy Ordered priest within the Reality which Christ instituted" (*Apostolicae Curae* # 31). In stark contrast, the religion of the Bishops' "New Mass" believes in "the community's memorial of Christ's Sacrifice as presided over by an episcopally commissioned presider or facilitator (the Bishops' "New Mass" collaborating cleric). This point is made absolutely clear in the chapter on Bugnini's institution of "New Mass." [N.P. In simple terms, one must always be aware of the Bishops' new definition and use of the word "sacrifice" in their services. Even though claiming their "New Mass" is Holy Sacrifice, it is not the Holy-Ordered, Christ-instituted Sacrifice of the Mass. At best, the Bishops' "New Mass" joyfully celebrates "the results" of the Sacrifice of Calvary. In the Catholic Mass, a properly functioning Holy Ordered priest "re-presents" the Holy Sacrifice of Calvary in an unbloody manner–the Holy Supper Sacrifice" (*The Mystery of Faith,* de la Taille, Book I, pp 154-161, Sheed & Ward, New York, 1940).

32. **Many of the more shrewd Anglican interpreters of the Ordinal have perceived the force of this argument, and they openly urge it against those who take the Ordinal in a new sense, and vainly attach to the Orders conferred thereby a value and efficacy which they do not possess. By this same argument is refuted the contention of those who think that the prayer, "Almighty God, giver of all good Things," which is found at the beginning of the ritual action, might suffice as a legitimate "form" of Orders, even in the hypothesis that it might be held to be sufficient in a Catholic rite approved by the Church.**

33. **With this inherent defect of "form" is joined the defect of "intention" which is equally essential to the Sacrament. The Church does not judge about the mind and intention, in so far as it is something by its nature internal; but in so far as it is manifested externally she is bound to judge concerning it. A person who has correctly and seriously used the requisite matter and form to effect and confer a sacrament is presumed for that very reason to have intended to do *(intendisse)* what the Church does. On this principle rests the doctrine that a Sacrament is truly conferred by the ministry of one who is a heretic or unbaptized, provided the Catholic rite be employed. On the other hand, if the rite be changed, with the manifest intention of introducing another rite not approved by the Church and of rejecting what the Church does, and what,**

by the institution of Christ, belongs to the nature of the Sacrament, then it is clear that, not only is the necessary intention wanting to the Sacrament, but that the intention is adverse to and destructive of the Sacrament.

Comment:
The Leonine Principle states that the Sacrament or Mass intended to be conferred or confected is *denied* when the Sacrament or Mass: "rite be changed with the manifest intention of introducing another rite not approved by the [One, Holy, Catholic and Apostolic] Church and of rejecting what [this] Church does and what, by institution of Christ [the Mass as instituted by Christ, not Bugnini] belongs to the nature of the Sacrament..." This evil intent has been disclosed and made evident to the effect that "New Mass" is to be considered *invalid.* "New Mass" is destructive to Christ's Holy Sacrifice of the Mass.

Perhaps a "simple equivalence" will help. As it were, (or, in effect) the Bishops have changed the Sacrament of Baptism to say: "We, the community, baptize you in our name." No Baptism happens. Similarly, as pointed out throughout this book, the Bishops have so changed the words of their "New Mass" as to render it no longer the Catholic Mass, but "sacrificially and sacramentally" *null and void.* Even the Bishops' own official definition of their "New Mass" attests to its invalidity as a communal celebration. Number 7 of the *Institutio*

Generalis Missali Romani, defines their "New Mass" as: "the sacred congregation, the gathering together of the People of God to celebrate under the leadership of the priest (presider) the Remembrance of the Lord."

34. **All these matters have been long and carefully considered by ourselves and by our venerable brethren, the Judges of the Supreme Council, of whom it has pleased Us to call a special meeting upon the 16th day of July last, the solemnity of Our Lady of Mount Carmel. They with one accord agreed that the question laid before them had been already adjudicated upon with full knowledge of the Apostolic See, and that this renewed discussion and examination of the issues had only served to bring out more clearly the wisdom and accuracy with which that decision had been made. Nevertheless, we deemed it well to postpone a decision in order to afford time both to consider whether it would be fitting or expedient that we should make a fresh authoritative declaration upon the matter, and to humbly pray for a fuller measure of divine guidance.**

35. **Then, considering that this matter, although already decided, had been by certain persons, for whatever reason, recalled into discussion, and that thence it might follow that a pernicious error would be fostered in the minds of many who might suppose that they possessed the Sacrament and effects of Orders, where these are nowise to be found, it seemed good to Us in the Lord to pronounce our judgment.**

36. **Wherefore, strictly adhering, in this matter, to the decrees of the pontiffs, our predecessors and confirming them most**

fully, and, as it were, renewing them by our authority, of our own initiative and certain knowledge, we pronounce and declare that ordinations carried out according to the Anglican rite have been, and are absolutely null and utterly void.

37. **It remains for Us to say that, even as we have entered upon the elucidation of this grave question in the name and in the love of the Great Shepherd, in the same we appeal to those who desire and seek with a sincere heart the possession of a hierarchy and of Holy Orders.**

38. **Perhaps until now aiming at the greater perfection of Christian virtue, and searching more devoutly the divine Scriptures, and redoubling the fervor of their prayers, they have, nevertheless hesitated in doubt and anxiety to follow the voice of Christ, which so long has interiorly admonished them. Now they see clearly whither He in His goodness invites them and wills them to come. In returning to His one only fold, they will obtain the blessings which they seek, and the consequent helps to salvation, of which He has made the Church the dispenser, and, as it were the constant guardian and promoter of His redemption amongst the nations. Then, indeed, "They shall draw waters in joy from the fountains of the Saviour," His wondrous Sacraments, whereby faithful souls have their sins truly remitted, and are restored to the friendship of God, are nourished and strengthened by the heavenly Bread, and abound with the most powerful aids unto their eternal salvation. May the God of peace, the God of all consolation, in His infinite tenderness enrich and fill with all these blessings those who truly yearn for them.**

40. **We decree that these letters and all things contained therein shall not be liable at any time to be impugned or objected to by reason of fault or any other defect whatsoever of subreption or of obreption of our intention, but are and shall be always valid and in force and shall be inviolably observed both juridically and otherwise, by all of whatsoever degree and preeminence, declaring null and void anything which, in these matters, may happen to be contrariwise attempted, whether wittingly or unwittingly, by any person whatsoever, by whatsoever authority or pretext, all things to the contrary notwithstanding.**

41. **We will that there shall be given to copies of these letters, even printed, provided that they be signed by a notary and sealed by a person constituted in ecclesiastical dignity, the same credence that would be given to the expression of our will by the showing of these presents. Given at Rome, at St. Peter's, in the year of the Incarnation of Our Lord, one thousand eight hundred and ninety-six, on the Ides of September, in the nineteenth year of our pontificate.**
–Leo PP. XIII

Concluding Comment:
By the authority of *Apostolicae Curae* ("always valid and in force") faithful Catholics are led to pronounce "null and void" or invalid, the Bishops' "New Mass" and "New Ordinal."

Papal Violation of *Apostolicae Curae*

As "post-Vatican II popes" often do, Pope Paul VI, by his gross failure to "properly pope," provides an example of how *Apostolicae Curae* is illustrated, *in effect,* by way of a violation of Apostolic Tradition. Even the title of one of his major talks exhibits both his enigmatic character and his diabolic intent: *"The Mass is the Same"* (Pope Paul VI, Nov. 19, 1969).

In this talk, he salutes the logon *"change;"* and, bows down in adoration of, and in abject submission to, those who *"Under a pretext of returning to the primitive form, corrupt the Liturgical Order in many ways to suit their* revolutionary errors" *(Apostolicae Curae);* all the while boldly claiming "the Mass is the same!" See his address below.

Our Dear Sons and Daughters:

1. **We wish to draw your attention to an event about to occur in the Latin Catholic Church: the introduction of the liturgy of the new rite of the Mass. It will become obligatory in Italian dioceses from the First Sunday of Advent, which this year falls on November 30. The Mass will be celebrated in a rather different manner from that in which we have been accustomed to celebrate it in the last four centuries, from the reign of St. Pius V, after the Council of Trent, down to the present.**

[Note: In fairness to Pope Paul VI, it must be emphasized that he *did not bindingly decree* the (Novus Ordo Liturgy) "New Mass" simulations as Canonized Masses. He merely observed that *"it will become obligatory."* ("Obligatory as what" we are not told.); "it is an act of obedience" (to Vatican II); and, "it is a step forward for her authentic tradition" – all declarative, but *not imperative* statements. We are confronted in this address with observations and *not binding legislations.*]

2. **This change has something astonishing about it, something extraordinary. This is because the Mass is regarded as the traditional and untouchable expression of our religious worship and the authenticity of our faith. We ask ourselves, how could such a change be made? What effect will it have on those who attend Holy Mass? Answers will be given to these questions, and to others like them, arising from this innovation. You will hear the answers in all the Churches. They will be amply repeated there and in all religious publications, in all schools where Christian doctrine is taught. We exhort you to pay attention to them. In that way, you will be able to get a clearer and deeper idea of the stupendous and mysterious notion of the Mass.**

3. **But in this brief and simple discourse We will try only to relieve your minds of the first, spontaneous difficulties which this change arouses. We will do so in relation to the first three questions which immediately occur to mind because of it.**

4. **How could such a change be made? Answer: It is due to the will expressed by the Ecumenical Council held not long ago. The Council decreed: "The rite of the**

Mass is to be revised in such a way that the intrinsic nature and purpose of its several parts, as also the connection between them, can be more clearly manifested, and that devout and active participation by the faithful can be more easily accomplished.

5. **"For this purpose the rites are to be simplified, while due care is taken to preserve their substance. Elements which, with the passage of time, came to be duplicated, or were added with but little advantage, are now to be discarded. Where opportunity allows or necessity demands, other elements which have suffered injury through accidents of history are now to be restored to the earlier norm of the Holy Fathers"** *(Sacrosanctum Concilium #50)*

6. **The reform which is about to be brought into being is therefore a response to an authoritative mandate from the Church. It is an act of obedience. It is an act of coherence of the Church with herself. It is a step forward for her authentic tradition. It is a demonstration of fidelity and vitality, to which we all must give prompt assent.**

7. **It is not an arbitrary act. It is not a transitory or optional experiment. It is not some dilletante's improvisation. It is a law. It has been thought out by authoritative experts of sacred liturgy; it has been discussed and meditated upon for a long time. We shall do well to accept it with joyful interest and put it into practice punctually, unanimously and carefully.**

8. **This reform puts an end to uncertainties, to discussions, to arbitrary abuses. It calls us back to that**

uniformity of rites and feeling proper to the Catholic Church, the hèir and continuation of that first Christian community, which was all "one single heart and a single soul" (Acts 4:32)**. The choral character of the Church's prayer is one of the strengths of her unity and her catholicit. The change about to be made must not break up that choral character or disturb it. It ought to confirm it and make it resound with a new spirit, the spirit of her youth.**

9. **The second question is: What exactly are the changes?**
Address of Pope Paul VI to a General Audience, Nov. 19, 1969, as reprinted from the English edition of *L'Osservatore Romano,* Nov. 27, 1969; brackets added.

This very allowance of a "significantly 'New Mass' rite" or a "man-made Mass-like ritual" (not originating from Apostolic Tradition into the Latin Rite according to the mind or spirit of Catholicism, but in direct contradiction to it) as reiterated and applied in *Apostolicae Curae,* assures us that the "new ritual" is null and void or invalid. "New Mass," is, therefore, conclusively invalid. Catholics faithful to the Sacred Heart of Jesus, the Holy Sacrifice of the Mass as instituted by Christ and celebrated by his faithful Holy Ordered priests in His Church, eagerly await the Bishops' "New Mass" being dogmatically decreed to be invalid.

CONCILIAR OR CATHOLIC?

Today we have the exact carbon copy of the situation St. Pius X described in 1903, where he made it clear that the promoters of error today are not found among our declared enemies –the promoters of error today are found in the very ranks of our own Church! Today we are witnessing that exact situation.

We are also witnessing the very thing which was predicted in Fatima in 1917. And I could see right up, it's not exactly making that public. But I don't pretend to have the text of that message of Our Blessed Mother in Fatima, but the text I received in Rome has a few paragraphs there which are still very much of interest. It was predicted then and it is happening now.

"A time of severe trial is coming for the Church. Not today, nor tomorrow," the Blessed Mother said in 1917, "but in the second half of the 20th century. Humanity will not develop as God desires it. Mankind will become sacrilegious and trample underfoot the gift it has received. No longer will order reign anywhere. "Even in the high places," the Blessed Mother predicted, "Satan will reign and direct the course of things. He will even succeed in infiltrating into the highest positions in the Church. Cardinals will oppose cardinals and bishops will oppose bishops. Satan will enter into their very midst. The Church will be obscured and all the world will be thrown into confusion."

Rev. Dr. Gommar de Pauw, *Conciliar or Catholic?*

Pope Paul VI, who promulgated the documents of the Council in 1965, began just three years later to reject the fruits of that Council, even associating it with the work of the Devil. He issued several startling statements to that effect.

> **The Church finds herself...in a...disturbed period of self-criticism...or self-destruction...It is as if the Church were attacking itself...It is as if the Church is destroying herself...**
>
> **Pope Paul VI, *Address to the Lombard Seminary*, 12/7/1968**

> **We have the impression that through some cracks in the wall, the smoke of Satan has entered the temple of God....**
>
> **Pope Paul VI, Sermon, Mass for Sts. Peter & Paul, 9th anniversary of his coronation, 6/29/1972**

> **Don't be surprised at Our answer and don't write it off as simplistic or even superstitious: one of the Church's greatest needs is to be defended against the evil we call the Devil.**
>
> **Pope Paul VI, General Audience, 11/15/1972**

> **The darkness of Satan has entered and spread throughout the Catholic Church even to its summit. Apostasy, the loss of the faith, is spreading throughout the world and into the highest level within the Church.**
>
> **Pope Paul VI, Address on 60th Anniversary of Fatima Apparitions, October 13, 1977**
>
> **The above quotes from: "What is the Authority of Vatican II?" www.traditio.com/tradlib/faq08.txt**

Chapter Fourteen

"CONSECRATION" PRAYERS CONCLUSIVELY INVALIDATE "NEW MASS"

The actual Consecration Prayers of the "New Mass" provide preponderance of evidence to conclude that "New Mass" is invalid.

Thinking as a Catholic, one refuses to determine Mass validity by considering "eight consecration words" as if Holy Mass were reduce-able to a "hocus pocus magic act." To determine validity, one even refuses to concentrate on the "twenty-two consecration words," which approach is also futile. The Anglican Liturgy (unlike the Bishops' New Liturgy) has faithfully translated these words ("*Hoc est Corpus Meum*" and "*Hic est...peccatorum.*"); yet, the Anglican "New Mass" has been dogmatically declared to be invalid.

Also, employment of Leonine Principles requires an evaluation of the "native character and spirit" (or religion) expressed (in or by all significant words and phrases) within any alleged Mass text. With the Canonized Latin Mass Text of the Catholic Mass as the standard, one is led to note how, (religiously) the Canonized Latin Mass Text has been altered. Any significant addition to; deletion from; or, modification of this standard text *ipso facto* invalidates (renders null and void) the purported Mass text. Furthermore, any such change could be introduced only with evil intent–ultimately, to reject the Mass as instituted by Christ and canonized by His Church (which is an act of apostasy by Christ and His Church).

Therefore, the standard Canonized Latin Mass Text with both the Anglican "New Mass" and the Bishops' "New Mass" texts in order to show that many religiously significant changes (additions, deletions or modifications relative to the Canonized Latin Mass Standard) have been made. Principally, one's concern focuses on all of the "words of Consecration," which words we now consider.

~~~~~~

I. CANONIZED LATIN MASS LITURGY
Qui *pridie, quam pateretur, accepit panem*
Who, the day he suffered the Oblation [into being] **He took bread**

I. BISHOPS' "NEW MASS" ENGLISH LITURGY 1997
The day before he suffered he took bread

I. ANGLICAN LITURGY 1549
who, in the same night that he was betrayed, took bread

~~~~~~

COMMENT

One is dealing with the most sacred words of the Consecration. Even a relatively proper exegesis/ translation of these words (if used by a Latin Rite priest to say Mass) would be gravely illicit and would most likely constitute invalidity. The Bishops' "New Mass" consecration prayers arebeyond being illicit translations. They are sacrilegious perversions. Once a priest says *"Qui"* or *"who"(*in the context of the Consecration prayer) he is thrown into being the *"who"* to whom he refers. He is forced into praying *ex officio in persona Christi,* as he must pray to effect a Holy Mass. Cardinal Ottaviani and his Cardinal theologians condemned the "New Mass" for refusing to bring the priest into "Christ-priest modality," observing, that the "New Mass" thus presented a mere narrative of a past event (thereby, invalidating their "New Mass"). Anglicans kept "who."

II. CANONIZED LATIN MASS LITURGY
in sanctas ac venerabiles manus suas, et elevatis oculis in coelum ad Te Deum patrem suum omnipotentem
into His holy and venerable hands, and having raised His eyes to heaven, unto Thee, O God, His Almighty Father,

II. BISHOPS' "NEW MASS" ENGLISH LITURGY 1997
and looking up to Heaven, to you His almighty Father,

II. ANGLICAN LITURGY 1549 no corresponding words

COMMENT

Both the Anglican Liturgy and the Bishops' "New Mass" English Liturgy "invalidate by omission." Why the deletions?

As Cardinal Ottaviani pointed out, in doing so, they reaffirm their denial of the "Holy Ordered Priesthood" and their desire to destroy "the Christ modality" by using a mere narrative tense to liturgize their apostasy. Both the Bishops' "New Mass" and the Anglican Service reject Holy-Ordered Priest as Christ-priest "presenting" the *here and now Salutary Event and Person.* At best, they merely recall to mind as a present blessing the past *once and forever over* salutary Calvary event.

The Bishops' and their "New Mass" reject the priest as being Christ-priest or as acting *ex officio in persona Christi.* Their liturgy is the action of the "people of God," not of the "Holy Ordered Priest."

Significantly, the Bishops's "New Mass" Liturgy purposely eliminates *"in sanctas ac venerabiles manus ejus...."* The Bishops' "New Mass" Service is in the hands of the facilitator, *not as Christ-priest,* but as the people's representative. Here lies one more proof that "New Mass" is invalid.

III. CANONIZED LATIN MASS LITURGY
Tibi gratias agens, benedixit,
Unto Thee, *gratias agens,* He blessed Hoc (into existence).
[*Hoc* is Christ's Body.]

III. BISHOPS' "NEW MASS" ENGLISH LITURGY 1997
He gave you thanks and praise. [no *blessed*]

III. ANGLICAN LITURGY 1549
and when he had blessed and given thanks (*blessed* is removed in modern Anglican Liturgy, since, as time goes on, protestant becomes more protestant and more like Newchurch's Novus Ordo perversion of the Catholic Mass).

COMMENT

The Bishops' "New Mass" Liturgy and the modernized Episcopalian or Anglican Liturgy omit *blessed.* Why? Christ-priest's unique role "to be" *the "Blesser" among us* in a salutary mystical/sacramental way is denied by protestants and the Bishops' "New Mass" heretics. At least, the Anglican Liturgy retained *blessed.* By doing so, the Anglican Liturgy, although invalid, was "far less a departure from" Catholicism than the Bishops' "New Mass" English Liturgy.

Note that there is no adequate translation for *gratias agens.* Literally, it means "[the Holy Ghost through

Holy Ordered Priest] doing graces;" or, the Holy Ghost accomplishing His Greatest Work within this age of the Holy Ghost. The sacred words of Consecration when uttered by a properly functioning Christ-priest bring into being the Realization of God's Saving Will as being the mystical/sacramental "work of" the Father (Who "blessed"); the Holy Spirit (Who "graces"); and the Son, (through Christ-priest's *dicens).* However, "New Mass" Bishops and their like-minded "priests" and people, with "deliberate sacrilege aforethought" reject a true Consecration for their "mock-masses.".

IV. CANONIZED LATIN MASS LITURGY

fregit deditque discipulis suis, dicens: Accipite, et manducate ex hoc omnes: HOC EST ENIM CORPUS MEUM.

He broke [HOC *–not it* and *not the bread*] and gave to His disciples saying: Take and eat of HOC, for HOC is my body [broken for you].

IV. BISHOPS' "NEW MASS" ENGLISH LITURGY 1997

He broke the bread and gave it to his disciples and said: Take this, all of you and eat it. This is my body.

IV. ANGLICAN LITURGY 1549

He brake it and gave it to his disciples saying, Take, eat [no it] this is my body, which is given for you: do this in remembrance of me.

COMMENT

Of primary importance is the fact, as determined by the

form (the words used) that the Bishops' "New Mass" Liturgy (according to the meaning of the words used) prays that "somehow, somewhat and perhaps not at all" the bread in some sense "is" and remains Christ *and bread.* This is proven by the very words used: "broke bread...this (bread) is my body." However, Christ-priest *blesses* (destroys bread) to create (or make present) HOC which is immediately defined: "Hoc est Corpus Meum." HOC is Christ's Body. HOC is not bread, is mystically broken (so as to effect Holy Sacrifice). The Bishops' "New Mass" is more evidently heretical than the dogmatically decreed "Anglican New Mass," which states that "it" which is broken is Christ's Body.

V. CANONIZED LATIN MASS LITURGY
Simili modo postquam coenatum est accipiens et hunc praeclarum Calicem in sanctas ac venerabiles manus suas: item tibi gratias agens,
In like manner, after supper, taking also this goodly chalice into His holy and venerable hands, again *gratias agens* unto Thee.

V. BISHOPS' "NEW MASS" ENGLISH LITURGY 1997
When supper was ended, he took the cup. Again he gave you thanks and praise.

V. ANGLICAN LITURGY 1549
Likewise, after supper, he took the cup, and when he had given thanks,

---

COMMENT

In both (the Bishops' "New Mass" and the Anglican Liturgy) the chalice of salvation is no longer considered a *goodly* cup; Christ's (and the "priest's") hands are no longer considered *holy* and *venerable.* The protestantly heretical narrative tense is employed. The Anglican is closer to thrusting the "priest" into the "supper verbal tense" than is "New Mass." The Anglican states *he had given* instead of (the "New Mass") *he gave* (which clearly refers to a *once and forever over with* event). Here and elsewhere, one perceives that the Bishops intend their liturgical presiders to function as narrators, not Holy Ordered Priests. Therefore, the Bishops' "New Ordinal 'priests'" cannot validly say a Canonized Latin Mass, even using the "Canonized Mass Text."

~~~~~~

VI. CANONIZED LATIN MASS LITURGY

gratias agens benedixit, deditque discipulis suis, dicens: Accipite, et bibite ex eo omnes:

***gratias agens,* He blessed and gave to His disciples saying: Take and drink of this:**

VI. BISHOPS "NEW MASS" ENGLISH LITURGY 1997

He [no *blessed]* gave the cup to his disciples and said: Take this all of you and drink from it,

VI. ANGLICAN LITURGY 1549

He gave it to them saying: [*said* in modern Anglican liturgies] Drink ye all of this;

~~~~~~

COMMENT

It would take us too far afield to bring out the reasons why *gratias agens* [doing graces] and *dicens* [saying] are used. However, they fulfil the first verses of the Bible. The Spirit acting on the waters represents the Holy Ghost acting on the bread and wine, as well as, those incorporated, or destined to be incorporated into Christ-Crucified (His Mystical Body) and, thereby, Christ-Glorified. *Dicens* is the Son speaking forth salvation both in Genesis and in every Salutary Event from the Last Supper, at each valid Mass and into the Eternal Mass, Heaven. All of this is the Salutary Will and Action of God the Father. In other words, *"mirabiliter reformasti"* is far more awesome than *"mirabiliter condidisti"* the paramount "work" of the Blessed Trinity. Christ and His Church tell us exactly how Christ wants "this" done on earth as in Heaven. Satan, through "New Mass, New Ordinal" Bishops, "sacrileges Christ's Saving Will."

With "tongue in cheek," one notes that the "dogmatically invalid" Anglican Liturgy is "less protestantly heretical" that the Bishops' "New Mass." At least, it retains *saying,* which word implies that somehow the Holy Supper Sacrifice is being repeated in our space and time. Such is Catholic dogma--the "saying of Holy Mass" by Christ-priest *ex officio in persona Christi.* The Bishops' "New Mass" liturgizes apostasy.

VII. CANONIZED LATIN MASS LITURGY

Hic est enim Calix Sanguinis mei, novi et aeterni testamenti: mysterium fidei: qui pro vobis et pro multis effundetur in remissionem peccatorum.

for this is the chalice of my Blood of the new and eternal covenant–the mystery of faith–which shall be shed for you and for many unto the forgiveness of sins.

VII. BISHOPS' "NEW MASS" ENGLISH LITURGY 1997

this is the cup of my blood of the new and everlasting covenant–the "mystery of faith" [was used in 1969, but was dropped by 1990]. It will be shed for you and for all [men–in 1969, not in 1990] so that sins may be forgiven.

VII. ANGLICAN LITURGY 1549

for this is My blood of the New Testament, which is shed for you and for many, for remission of sins:

COMMENT

Again, the Bishops' "New Mass" Liturgy is more protestant and, consequently, clearly "deeper into apostasy" and "more evidently invalid" than the Anglican Liturgy. *For* is omitted from the Bishops' "New Mass" Liturgy. Also, the Anglican retains *many*. "New Mass" inserts *all* and thus, according to every reputable theologian, invalidates (makes impossible) its Service being *the effective Salutary Action or Event of Mass. All* are not saved. Such blatant heresy cannot "make a Mass."

Initially, "New Mass" used "all men;" but, by 1990, the custodians of the "New Mass" Liturgical sacrilege realized that this passage was "politically offensive." ***"All men"*** **was changed to the more politically correct** ***"all."*** **Also, for sacrilegious reasons, "New Mass" revisionists dropped "the priest's doing into** ***mysterium fidei,"*** **and made it instead "the people's doing."** ***"Let us proclaim the mystery of faith"*** **was invented. "New Mass" mocks Christ. The Bishops officially reject the Holy Ordered priesthood and has the people dare to proclaim into being the Mystery of Faith. "New Mass" is grossly apostate. Also, "New Mass" implicitly, but clearly, denies Christ's Sacramental Presence, as it proclaims:** ***"Christ has died, Christ has risen. Christ will come again."*** **Christ, sacramentally Present, is purposely omitted and thus denied.** ***Why?*** **Obviously, "New Mass" rejects transubstantiation.**

With sacrilege aforethought, Bishops "liturgically teach" that the "people celebrate Mass." No longer are they Catholics who believe in and "liturgize" the exclusive celebration of Holy Mass by Holy Ordered Priest. Also, "New Mass" positively expresses and professes its heretical, sacrilegious notion of priesthood: "We the people bring mystery of faith into being by the people's proclamation rite." A similar heresy-based apostasy is repeated at communion as each communicant proclaims himself "body of Christ" by his "Amen" or "so be it." Indeed, "New Mass" Liturgy is far more obviously invalid than the dogmatically proclaimed invalid Anglican Liturgy (according to *Apostolicae Curae's* principle that an alien "native character and spirit" nullifies or invalidates).

VIII. CANONIZED LATIN MASS LITURGY
Haec quotiescumque feceritis, in Mei Memoriam facietis.
As often as you shall do this, do into My Memory

VIII. BISHOPS' "NEW MASS" ENGLISH LITURGY 1997
As often as you do this, do it in memory of me

VIII. ANGLICAN LITURGY 1549
Do this, as oft as you shall drink it, in [*in* replaced by *for* in modern Anglican Liturgy] **remembrance of me.**

COMMENT

Hesitating to translate the most sacred and inviolable words of the Canon and, especially, the Consecration, I do so, only to point out gross sacrilege committed by inventors of a radically new and alien liturgy. Let's note one last thing. This phrase does not mean *"do it in memory of me."* [That's why the Bishops' "New Mass" did not bother to translate *"in memoriam"* as it is: "into the Memory (Christ)".]

The "New Mass" sacrilegious rendition is protestant, meaning "we merely recall the Last Supper." For them, "Mass" is not Christ's Holy Order empowered mystical/sacramental "re-doing" into His Memory. The Bishops' "New Mass," as the Anglican, rejects the "here and now 'effective' Holy Sacrifice." For both of these heretical apostates, their liturgical services are, at best, recollections or remembrances of the past and forever over with Sacrifice of Christ at Calvary which is "universally effective" for the Bishops and "selectively effective" for "less apostate" Anglicans.

As defined by the Councils of Florence and Trent, each Holy Sacrifice of Mass is *effective unto salvation.* The Holy Sacrifice of Mass brings and sustains the Elect into *the Memory, Christ.* As it were, each Mass does *or effects* the Elect into Christ's Salutary Deed into *the Memory, Who is Christ.* Each valid Mass is the Essence of the Holy Supper Sacrifice brought into Christ-priest's space/time.

Each valid Mass is Christ's totally effective Holy Sacrifice repeated in a mystical/sacramental manner. Each Mass, as the Canonized Eastern Masses bring out, is somehow entrance into Heaven: "Blessed is the Kingdom of the Father, the Son and the Holy Ghost."

♦ CONCLUSION

An objective comparison of the Consecration prayers of the Canonized Latin Mass with the Anglican and Bishops' "New Mass" equivalents, in the light of Leonine principles, leads one to conclude that the Bishops' "New Mass" is invalid since Anglican Liturgy which is far less apostate or protestant was dogmatically decreed to be invalid. A critic may be led to contend that I am "reading in" heresy-based apostasy.

However, as *Apostolicae Curae* pointed out, the burden of proof to the contrary automatically falls upon the critic, who might object to such conclusions. Why? The canonized standard is just that.

Any significant deviation from this standard: (1) implies evil intent; (2) is sacrilegious; (3) if "significant" renders the perpetrators heretics; and (4) if persisted in and made into a "New Mass," renders the perpetrators full-fledged apostates. To be saved from eternal Hell, (to be "un-anathematized") such liturgical apostates must return to Catholicism, to the exclusive use of Canonized Mass Texts, as well as, compliance to all other seriously binding Catholic liturgical laws and dogmas.

Chapter Fifteen

"OFFERTORY" PRAYERS CONCLUSIVELY INVALIDATE "NEW MASS"

"Now let us understand what was done by the English Reformers in the New Liturgy drawn up in 1549 to take the place of the ancient Mass. In a general way, it may be said that up to the Gospel, this liturgy of the new order followed outwardly at least, the old Missals.

The offering of Christ, the Immaculate Victim, along with the offertory prayers expressing oblation and sacrifice–a part which was known as the Offertory–were swept away altogether in the New Liturgy. In their place was substituted a few sentences appropriate to almsgiving and a *new meaning* was given to the word *Offertory,* which has since come to signify an offering of praise along with our gifts–bread, wine, etc. – to God. This change is significant of the 'Eucharistic' doctrines of the German Reformers.

Abbot Gasquet, *Advent Sermons,* 1913, as quoted in *The Abbot & Me On Liturgy,* Fr. Paul Trinchard, pp. 27-28

The Bishops "New Mass" has "out-protestantized" the Anglicans, replacing the Catholic (or orthodox) Offertory with a sophisticated, antique meal blessing. Besides this, the Bishops also "bastardized and mollified" the "pre-Offertory" (a.k.a. Mass of the

Catechumens or Liturgy of the Word) Bible readings, formal prayers and versicals to express the Bishops' unique religion in their "New Mass". The International Commission for English Liturgy (ICEL) implemented the Bishops' wishes within the English-speaking world. Such butchering of God's Word and of other Mass versicles (by the concerted efforts of hundreds of men throughout the world) mollified negative salutary fundamentals (sin, Hell, etc.); and, superficialized and sensualized positive salutary fundamentals; while perverting the Bible into being "Godly words no longer applicable as God intended." (See *God's Word,* MAETA.)

As regards what is referred to as 'the liturgy of the Eucharist," one observes the Bishops' rejection or sacrilegious perversion of the Offertory Prayers and Ritual. Both the Anglican and the Bishops' "New Mass" movements rejected Holy Mass as essentially being Christ's Salutary Offering or Oblation and the Elects' oblation in, into and *through Christ's Oblation.* Martin Luther proclaimed *"Tolle Missam, tolle ecclesiam."* The Bishops' Liturgical Revolt developed and implemented its own comparable logon (in the vernacular, of course):

> **"Take away the Offertory, destroy the Mass and create the New Mass, New Order Services."**
>
> **Bishops' Liturgical Revolt, 1960's–present**

By way of opposition to “New Mass” “theology” or homology, Catholic Dogma is cited:

> **“In other words, although there are as many Sacrifices as there are Mass Offertories, at the same time, there does exist a real oneness between them and the One Offering and Offered on the Cross, as well as, at the Last Supper and eternally in Heaven.”**
>
> **Council of Trent, Sess**

The Anglican and the Bishops’ “New Masses” reject the “Holy Ordered Priesthood” as dogmatically defined by the Council of Trent. Both Anglican and “New Mass” Novus Ordo liturgical apostates reject the Holy Ordered Christ-priest and his Offertory of the Canonized Latin Mass Liturgy; thereby, they invalidate “their Consecration” by perverting it into being merely a narrative of the Last Supper. (See *The Abbot & Me On Liturgy,* Cardinal Gasquet, 2002, as well as, *The Critical Study of the Novus Ordo,* Cardinal Ottaviani, et al, 1970.)

The liturgical revolutionaries of both Anglican and the Bishops’ “New Mass,” contend, in effect, that “the offerings of each Mass and the offering at the Last Supper are as unrepeatable as the offering at Calvary; consequently, the Mass is not the Holy Sacrifice realized in our midst.” In effect, these revolutionaries merely “solemnly” narrate the Supper and recall “Bloody Calvary.” They fail to say the Mass as instituted by Christ, and thereby, they have no Mass. They have a “fake mass,” an unholy sacrilege,” an “invalid Mass.”

Clearly, the Anglican and the Bishops'"New Mass" services, especially, in the offertory formulae, sacrilege and invalidate the Mass of Apostolic Tradition, which was instituted by Christ. Consequently, both religions reject Holy Orders as defined by Christ and His *semper ubique idem* Church. *Apostolicae Curae* dogmatized this as fiducial fact and implicitly dogmatized the principle that invalid services produce and come from invalid ordinals and vice versa. *Lex orandi, lex credendi et vice-versa.*

It is obvious to any impartial observer that the religion of the Bishops "New Mass" Liturgy has its presider offer to God, bread and wine, (not Christ, Immaculate Victim). Sacrilegiously, the "offering prayers" of the Novus Ordo "New Mass" offer bread and wine, not Christ. This constitutes the Abominable Desolation, the unholy in the place of the Most Holy.

"New Mass" *Offering* Is a Jewish Non-Salutary Ritual

The "New Mass" Offertory is sacrilegious (and thus invalid) by reason of its effective rejection of Christ's Salutary Oblation. In place of the Catholic Offertory (Christ's Salutary Oblation) "New Mass" substitutes a "Christ-less" offering. When one researches the origin of, and/or inspiration for, the "New Mass" "Offering Prayers," one discovers that they mimic the following Jewish Kabbala Prayers. These "Christ-less" and "non-salutary" meal blessing prayers are given to us in the language of that time, Latin.

~~~~~~

"Blessing for the bread: *'Benedictus tu, Domine Deus noster, mundi Domine qui panem nobis a terra produxisti.'*
[Blessed art thou our Lord and God, thou art Lord of the world. Thou hast given to us this bread from the earth.]

Blessing for the wine: *'Benedictus tu, Domine Deus noster, mundi Domine qui vineae fructum creaveris.'*
[Blessed....world. Thou has made this fruit of the vine.]"
From *The Jewish Kabbala,* cited by Jean Basdorf, *Synagogue Judaica,* 1661, p .24-25

~~~~~~

As one can prove to himself, within the Novus Ordo Service, the facilitator, presider or community rep gives a "non-Holy Ordered" type of blessing to bread and wine in order to "spiritualize" (not consecrate) them. In "the context of Mass," this "blessing" is gross sacrilege. In contrast, the Christ-instituted Offertory begins:

***"Suscipe sancte Pater hanc immaculatam hostiam...* Accept, O Holy Father the Immaculate Victim [Christ]..."**

This Offertory Prayer both activates the priest to be Christ-priest (to act officially *in persona Christi* (in the person of Christ); and indicates that Christ is the One

Who offers and is offered as *Immaculatam Hostiam* (Immaculate Victim) for sin. How? Christ acts through His Christ-priest, who *ex officio,* (carrying out the duty of his work as Christ-priest) acts (speaks and does) *in persona Christi* (representing Christ). Never does Christ-priest act (as in New Order "New Mass" services) in the name of, and by virtue of, the commissioning given him to be a presider or facilitator by the community of "believers" or as "an overseer" in the name of, or with power from, "the faith community."

Christ-priest "Ex Officio" Acts "In Persona Christi"

> **"For the Victim is one and the same, the same now *offering* by the ministry of priests, who once *offered* Himself on the Cross, the manner of *offering* alone being different." In other words, although there are as many sacrifices as there are *Offertories,* at the same time, there does exist a real oneness between them and the One *Offering* and *Offered* on the Cross, as well as, at the Last Supper and eternally in Heaven."**
>
> **Council of Trent, Sess. 22**

Every Catholic must believe in the (temporal and eternal) Mass as being Christ's Salutary Offering of Holy Supper and of Calvary: "the manner of offering alone being different; at Mass (as at the Supper) unbloody; at Calvary, bloody." Every valid Mass repeats (and thus brings about so as to be made present again) Christ's Last Supper Oblation brought into here and now mystical/sacramental being through Christ-priest by the awesome power of the Holy Spirit. Mass ritual was instituted by Christ to "make present once again" Christ's Salutary Offering which, being totally effective, is the Elects' salutary oblation into and through Christ. The Mass Ritual of Salutary Oblation (in order to be valid and sinless) must be done as specified by Christ through His *semper ubique idem* Church, as found in the Deposit of Faith.

Each temporal Mass repeats the Offering of the Last Supper as spelled out by Christ and canonized by His Church. At each valid Mass, the Christ-instituted, Church-canonized way of "redoing" the essence of the Last Supper by a validly facultied Christ-priest, is so "God-powerful" that it realizes the Salutary Will on earth as it is realized eternally in Heaven. Therefore, to add to, to delete or modify any Christ-instituted and Church-given "Apostolic Tradition defined" way to bring this Most Holy Reality into being blasphemes God; constitutes mega-sacrilege; and, according to Pope St. Pius V's dogmatic decree, such "sacrileging prelates (including popes)" will bring upon themselves "the wrath of almighty God."

(cf. *The Mystery of Faith,* Fr. de la Taille, S.J. See also *Quo Primum.*)

Crisis of the Holy See

As far back as 1861, Cardinal Manning saw very clearly that the cessation of the Holy Mass was coming, having read carefully the writings of the Fathers on this subject from the earliest times. This great Cardinal gives us the following insired predictions:

> **"The holy Fathers who have written upon the subject of anti-Christ, and of the prophecies of Daniel, without a single exception, as far as I know–and they are the Fathers both of the East and of the West, the Greek and the Latin Church–all of them unanimously–say that in the latter end of the world, during the reign of anti-Christ, the Holy Sacrifice of the Altar will cease. In the work on the end of the world, ascribed to St. Hippolytus, after a long description of the afflictions of the last days, we read as follows:**
>
> **'The Churches shall lament with a great lamentation, for there shall be offered no more oblation nor worship acceptable to God. The sacred buildings of the churches shall be as hovels; and the precious Body and Blood of Christ shall not be manifest in those days; the true Liturgy shall become extinct...Such is the universal testimony of the Fathers of the early centuries.'"**

***Crisis of the Holy See,* 1861**

Chapter Sixteen

“NEW ORDINAL” ALLEGED “PRIESTS” ARE CONCLUSIVELY INVALID

Since the Ordinal defines the Service and vice versa, the New “Ordinals” themselves are as invalid as the “New Mass.” See *Apostolicae Curae* and *The Abbot & Me on Liturgy.*

What is the immutable and *sine qua non* essence of Holy Ordered Priesthood? Why is a man made a priest in the Catholic Church?

Answer: Primarily and essentially, a man receives Holy Orders to offer the Holy Sacrifice of the Mass and administer the priest-dependent sacraments. The traditional Rite of Ordination explains this clearly. In the Church-given words of the Bishop to the ordinand, the office of the priesthood is explained according to the traditional understanding of what a priest should be:

> **Dearly beloved son, as you are now about to be consecrated to the office of the Priesthood, endeavor to receive it worthily, and when you have received it, fulfill its duties blamelessly. The Priest is ordained to offer Sacrifice, to bless, to guide, to preach and to baptize. With great awe should one advance to so high a state...”**

The Bishops' "New Mass" and "New Ordinal" imply an alien religion.It is apostate! The Bishops'"New Ordinal" betrays its anti-Catholic and anti-Christ religion from the beginning of its "commissioning rite." Here is how the Office of the Priesthood is explained by the Bishop according to the 1978 rite:

> **My son, you are now to advance to the order of the presbyterate. You must apply your energies to the duty of teaching in the name of Christ, the chief Teacher. Share with mankind the word of God you have received with joy. Meditate on the law of God, believe what you read, teach what you believe, and put into practice what you teach...In the memorial of the Lord's death and resurrection, make every effort to die to sin and to walk in the new life of Christ.**

Obviously, the Bishops' collaborators, presiders or facilitators are not ordained as Holy Ordered Priests.

> **"Today we find men of intelligence and good faith claiming to have the same Christ-given sacrifice and the same sacrificing priests as the Catholic Church, while they are using a new man-made liturgy from which, of set purpose, every notion of Oblation and Sacrifice has been ruthlessly removed, and their ministers are ordained by an Ordinal, which designedly was composed to express the rejection of the sacrificial character of the Catholic priest. The prayer for Christian Unity must go up from every heart, but if it is to be something more than sentiment, facts must be faced and resolved honestly."** Abbot Gasquet, "4th Advent Sermon," 1913, Chairman of *Apostolicae Curae*, *Commission*, See *Abbot & Me On Liturgy,* Fr. Paul Trinchard.

The facts which prove or show forth the "invalidating characteristics" of the Novus Ordo or "New Mass" Ordinal (but not proper theological reasoning concerning this ordinal) can be found in Michael Davies' *Order of Melchisedek.* This book manifests the intent of today's Revolting Bishops (of the Novus Ordo "New Mass" Liturgy) to make certain *"their ministers are ordained by an Ordinal which designedly was composed to express the rejection of the sacrificial character of the Catholic priest."* [Cardinal Gasquet, describing the Anglican Ordinal. All the more so, his remarks apply today to the Bishops' "New Ordinal."]

Shortly after introducing their new services, the Anglican Bishops introduced a matching or "religiously compatible" ordinal. So too, the Bishops' revolting against the Catholic Church in the 1960's also developed a religiously compatible ordinal to match their Novus Ordo "New Mass." The "New Mass" began in 1966. The "New Ordinal" was introduced in 1969.

The native character and spirit of the Anglican Ordinal led to its dogmatic condemnation. The native character and spirit of the Revolting Bishops "New Ordinal" is far more protestant than that of the Anglican Ordinal. This fact forces a faithful Catholic to pronounce it to be "conclusively invalid." This conclusion becomes necessary once one realizes the gravity of "what has been deleted."

Invalidating Omissions

"Every prayer in the traditional rite which stated specifically the essential role of a priest as a man ordained to offer propitiatory sacrifice for the living and dead has been removed" [from the ordinal]. ***The Order of Melchizedek,*** **Michael Davies**

With "invalidating and malicious intent," prayers such as the following were deleted with only one possible intention–to insure that the Revolting Bishops' "New Mass" presiders and collaborators would not receive the Sacrament of Holy Orders:

✘ "Theirs be the task to change with blessing undefiled, for the service of thy people, bread and wine into the Body and Blood of Thy Son." **(Abolished)**

✘ "Receive the power to offer sacrifice to God, and to celebrate Mass, both for the living and the dead, in the name of the Lord." **(Abolished)**

✘ "The blessing of God Almighty, the Father, the Son and the Holy Ghost come down upon you, and make you blessed in the priestly Order, enabling you to offer propitiatory sacrifices for the sins of the people to Almighty God." **(Abolished)**

The Bishops' "New Ordinal" and "New Mass" were fabricated by the same anti-Christ and anti-Church alleged "experts." Pope Paul VI's (1969) New Ordination Rite was created with the help of Annibale Bugnini and six Protestant ministers who designed the "New Mass." Their fabricated "New Ordination Rite" is compatible with the spirit and religion of the "New Mass Liturgy."

As a consequence, "Holy Ordered Priesthood" would cease and desist. From that which was "omitted" in their "New Ordinal" (compared to the Catholic Rite), it is obvious that the Bishops purposed to commisssion episcopal collaborators and liturgical presiders (or designated receivers of the gifts of the people). In so doing, they purposely rejected any "expressed possibility" of ordaining a "Holy Ordered Priest," or, of continuing the Holy Ordered Priesthood as defined by Christ in the Holy Bible and in Apostolic Tradition.

That which was added [the insertion of a non-Catholic, anti-Catholic form: (the words used, which are at odds with the Catholic Standard)] attests to the Bishops' intent. Just as the words (thus the intent) of their "New Mass," cannot effect "Sacrifice and Sacrament," likewise, the words (thus the intent) of their "New Ordinal," cannot possibly *(in se)*"effect" the Sacrament of Holy Orders, *thus excluding the possibility of ordaining a Holy Ordered Priest.*

"Nothing is more dangerous than the heretics who...corrupt with a single word, like a drop of poison, the purity and simplicity of the faith which we have received through tradition from God and through the Apostles."

Pope Leo XIII, who decreed Anglican "New Ordinal" invalid.

The methodology employed in *Apostolicae Curae* by Pope Leo XIII to dogmatically pronounce judgment that the Anglican Ordinals and Services are invalid is the same thus applied to the Bishops' "New Mass" and "New Ordinal." This methodology applied to the Anglican, applies, *a fortiori* to the Bishops' "New Mass" and "New Ordinal" to the same conclusive effect: the form (or new words) as used, do not effect (or bring about) Holy Ordered Priests, (but merely, presiders or receivers of the gifts"); thereby, the "effect" is an apostate church body (which is not Catholic).

As with Anglican Ordinals, the Bishops' "New Ordinal" expresses and produces an apostate religion. Pope Leo employed the principle that Services determine Ordinals and vice-versa: an invalid Service ("New Mass") "requires" and thus, "begets" an invalid Ordinal (and vice versa).

By modifying: adding to; subtracting from the standard Canonized Latin Rite Ordinal, invalidity was assured. Heresy, liturgized, "begets" apostasy.

Why Ordain?

One wonders why the need exists, or why the Bishops even bother to "ordain" New Age "priests," since their "New Mass" and "new religion" professes that *all* are such: "All celebrate"? In the reality and substance of Catholic teaching, the Revolting Bishops' alleged "ordination" gives out commissions to preside over or to facilitate community worship; as well as, to be episcopal collaborators. These men (so far, it's only men) also become "embryonic bishops" most of whom will be aborted before "being born as bishops."

Pope Leo XIII dogmatically declared the Anglican Services "null and void" because of invalid "ordinals." The Revolting Bishops' "New Ordinal" is far more protestant than their Anglican counterparts. *A fortiori,* to a faithful Catholic, they are conclusively invalid. Faithful Catholics now eagerly await their being dogmatically declared to be such.

Pope Pius XII

Pope Pius XII, as Secretary of State, confided the following to Count Galeazzi:

"Suppose, dear friend, that Communism was only the most visible of the instruments of subversion to be used against the Church and the traditions of Divine Revelation...I am worried by the Blessed Virgin's messages to Lucia of Fatima. This persistence of Mary about the dangers which menace the Church is a Divine warning against the suicide of altering the Faith, in its liturgy, its theology and its soul." –Msgr. Roche

"A day will come when the civilized world will deny its God. When the Church will doubt as Peter doubted. She will be tempted to believe that man has become God...in our churches Christians will search in vain for the red lamp where God awaits them, like Magdalen weeping before the empty tomb, they will ask, 'Where have they taken Him?'"
Msgr. Roche, "Pie XII devant l'histoire" pp. 52-53.

PART THREE

THE NATURE OR PURPOSE OF "NEW MASS"

"The cock will crow..." Christ's prediction to Peter.
"Peter betrays Christ. Pope & Bishops betray Christ."

"Considering all these things, there is good reason to fear...this great perversity–the substitution of man for God–may be...the beginning of those evils reserved for the last days, and the 'son of perdition' (2 Thess 2:3) of whom the Apostle speaks, may already be in the world. In very truth, we cannot think otherwise in virtue of the audacity and wrath employed...in persecuting religion, in combating the dogmas of faith, in the firm determination of uprooting and destroying all relations between man and the Divinity. Moreover...this is the distinguishing mark of the anti-Christ, with unlimited boldness man has put himself in place of God, exalting himself above all that is called God...in such a way that although he cannot utterly extinguish in himself all knowledge of God, he has condemned God's majesty and made the universe a temple in which he himself is to be adored. 'He sits in the temple of God, showing himself as if he were God' (2Thess 2:4)."

Pope St. Pius X, *E Supremi Apostolatus, #5,*Oct. 4, 1903.

Birth of the Schismatic Heretical Church in the U.S.

It was in the year, 1962, that a schismatic heretical Conciliar sect of the Church in the U.S. was born. Why? Because, regardless of the clear solemn oath of Pope John XXIII, the majority of our American bishops refused to obey.

> **"We in Rome cannot possibly permit you American bishops to use this kind of Mass formula."....**

At one time, that would have been the final decision and any Catholic bishop would have submitted immediately. No longer....In Rome itself...where he was to attend the opening Council of the Synod of Bishops last September 29 (1966), Archbishop Deardon of Detroit, in his capacity as president of the American Catholic Bishops, publicly announced that, even though Rome had rejected this English text of the Canon, we in the United States make it now mandatory in all public Masses and we will not even wait until December 3, the day we originally planned. We will do it immediately, as soon as the printing can be done. And that's why they made it mandatory on October 22nd. Now, if that isn't an open schism, then I don't know what a schism is......

....I should know because I was there on the faculty at the time. And I had instructions from our Bishop in Baltimore NOT to implement the constitution from Rome. That's when I resigned.

Rev. Dr. Gommar de Pauw, *Conciliar or Catholic?*, 1967, www.traditio.com

Chapter Seventeen

THE BIBLE PREDICTS THE "NEW ORDER" LITURGY AND GOVERNMENT

> **"I saw a Second Beast rise out of the earth. It has two 'horns' like a lamb, but it spoke like a dragon. It exercises authority with the First Beast and makes the earth and its people to worship the First Beast. It worked great signs, even making fire come down from heaven...It deceives those who dwell on earth...It slew those who would not worship the image of the Beast...the number of the Beast is the number of Man (666)."** Apoc 13:11-18, my version

Regarding the Third Secret, Sr. Lucia of Fatima refers us to the 12th and 13th chapters of the Apocalypse. The 12th chapter reveals Our Lady birthing Christ, Sacrifice and Sacrament, as "the life-force" of Mary's Elect Remnant. The 13th chapter reveals anti-Christ and treats of the two Beasts of the Apocalypse, born of Satan.

Having been cast down upon the earth, Satan eventually brings forth the First and Second Beasts of the Apocalypse. The New Age and the New Order (the Novus Ordo) come from Satan. Increasingly, this world, which already lies in Satan's lap (1 Jo 5:19) will be under his control (Apoc 13).

The First Beast is the rule or government of man by man according to man's "God-less" standards, as "inspired or concocted by" Satan and his spirits. The Second Beast is the Bishops' "New Mass" as expressed in its liturgy, which celebrates and worships man as if he were God (cf. Gn 3).

The Second Beast looking like a lamb, spoke like a dragon (Apoc 13:11). Similarly, the Bishops' existential church speaks "spiritually," as "New Mass" appears to be the lamb slain, but witnesses to the devil. These are informed by the spirit of anti-Christ, exalting man and man's will; and, dethroning God and His Will. "New Mass" Liturgy even redefines liturgy as "man's doing his thing" rejecting the Catholic definition: "praising God the God-given way."

What is the characteristic of the Second Beast? It deceitfully appears to be the lamb, but it is satanic. "New Mass" appears to be and proclaims itself as being to all appearances "like a lamb," or "the Lamb slain," the Holy Mass; but, the "New Mass" is deceptively satanic, since it is a mockery and sacrilege of the Holy Mass. It is the unholy in the place of the Most Holy. This is the Abominable Desolation–the Most Holy sacrileged into the unholy.

The "New Mass" Liturgy Predicted

Jesus was once asked: *"What shall be the sign of thy coming, and of the end of the world?* (Matt 24:3)"

> **"When you therefore shall see the abomination of desolation, which was spoken of by Daniel the prophet, standing in the holy place: he that readeth, let him understand. (Matt 24:3)."**

According to Pope Leo XIII, the "Abominable Desolation" describes "the worst possible lacking"– the replacement of the Most Holy with the unholy– both liturgically and as referring to the papal throne (as apparent in his Leonine Prayer to St. Michael). Also, when this reference is researched, in the Anchor or Jerusalem Bible, note that the "Abomination of Desolation" can be considered as an object: a second altar erected "upon" and "opposed to" the altar of God (1 Macc 1:57) (1 Macc 1:62). Typically, in the Old Dispensation, it applied to a specific period in the history of the Jewish Temple. It referred to a false and idolatrous form of worship introduced in substitution of the true sacrifice, at a general time of apostasy of Jewry from their received faith. This object (false altar) will be in one of "the wings of the Temple" (Dan 9:27). This "wing" can be interpreted as being the Latin Rite of the Catholic Church.

"Upon and Opposed To"

In a wide sense of the word, the Sanctuary constitutes the Altar of God. Originally, the Novus Ordo "New Mass" table was placed in the Sanctuary or "upon the Altar." Also, it "opposed the true Altar." It stood in opposition to the true Altar, as well as, "opposite" the true Altar within the Sanctuary. It "fits prophecy." It is the "Abomination of Desolation" [the absence of God--when God is presumed to be present; is yet related to as being present, but is not].

Abominable Desolation

The original abomination, as well as, the "New Mass" abomination are both uniquely characterized by "liturgically active females." In the times of the Abominable Desolation, women are in the Sanctuary during Divine Liturgy.

> **"At no time in Jewish history were women involved in Jewish liturgical practices except at the time of the 'Abomination of Desolation;' and then, they were all over the altar."**
>
> ***Bible Commentary* on 2 Macc 6:4**

> **"These most crafty enemies have filled and inebriated with gall and bitterness, the Church, the spouse of the immaculate Lamb, and have laid impious hands on her most sacred possessions. In the Holy Place itself, where has been set up the see of the most Holy Peter, and the Chair of Truth, for the light of the world, they have raised the throne of their abominable impiety; with the iniquitous design, that when the Pastor has been struck, the sheep may be scattered."**
>
> **Pope Leo XIII**

What Satan began by the Protestant Revolt, he is now bringing to perfection through the Bishops' Liturgical Revolt. Luther vowed to destroy Holy Church by destroying Holy Mass: *"Tolle missam, tolle ecclesiam!"* Now Luther's satanic desire, has been fulfilled. Holy Mass has been forbidden from the Roman Rite of the establishment church by its own Bishops! The grossly unholy "New Order" "New Mass" dispensation now stands in the place of the Most Holy Salutary Dispensation, (Sacrifice and Sacrament) God's greatest Gift to sinful men.

The Desolation (lack of Holy Mass) is made abominable by the substitution of a fake and sacrilegious service in place of Holy Mass. We now suffer the Abominable Desolation (2 Macc 6:4) as predicted by Pope Leo XIII: *"abominable impiety is enthroned in Rome and flows from Rome (to all appearances)."*

Cardinal Gasquet on the Anglican"New Order Mass"

The Canon of the New Service or New Order was, so far as ideas go, an alien invention by men. It is impossible for any unbiased mind to compare the ancient Canon ot the Holy Mass...with the New Liturgy, without seeing that both in spirit and substance it was conceived with the design of getting rid of the Catholic Mass altogether. It was as little a translation of the Latin Missal as the similar Lutheran productions of Germany, which were ostensibly based upon the design of getting rid of the sacrificial character of the Mass altogether.

To anyone who will put the one [liturgy] by the side of the other and note te changes and omissions, it must appear as clear as the noonday sun that there is an essential and substantial difference between the two liturgies.

Radical religious changes were made. They reflect and teach an essential denial of Catholic dogma.

***Advent Sermons,* 1913, St. Patrick's Church, New York, Aidan Cardinal Gasquet, head of Pope Leo XIII's Commission on the Anglican Liturgy, 1896. See *Apostolicae Curae &Abbot & Me On Liturgy,* MAETA.**

Chapter Eighteen

"NEW MASS" REPLACES HOLY MASS

> **"....With unlimited boldness man has put himself in place of God, exalting himself above all that is called God. He has done this in such a way that although he cannot utterly extinguish in himself all knowledge of God, he has condemned God's majesty and made the universe a temple in which he himself is to be adored. 'He sits in the temple of God, showing himself as if he were God' (2Thess 2:4)."**
> **Pope St. Pius X, inaugural encyclical, *E Supremi Apostolatus, #5,* Oct. 4, 1903**

Both Pope St. Pius X and Pope Leo XIII direct us to realize that the Apocalyptic Church or "a false church" will replace God with "man." Essentially, this religion is the dethronement of God and the enthronement of man, as equivalent to Christ or God.

A peculiar zeitgeist has led churchmen to wholeheartedly abandon Christ as "first served;" to fabricate; to implement and to impose the alien "New Mass" Liturgy upon the people of God. The "New Mass" was born from the disobedient spirit of Vatican Two. In "New Mass," the Second Beast (Apoc 13) is given liturgical expression. Man as he is, with

his feelings and desires, is to be enthroned according to the pattern created by reigning apostate "experts." In addressing the United Nations, Pope Paul VI put "this church" at the service of mankind (at the service of the new age). Furthermore, his closing speech at Vatican Two (December 1965) stated:

> **"The religion of God made man** [Christ's religion] **has come up against the religion of man who makes himself God. And what happened? ....in our new humanism: we, also, we, more than anyone else, have the cult of man..."**
>
> **Pope Paul VI, *Catholic Documents,* Jan. 1966**

A "new religion" was born as God was dethroned and man enthroned. The existential church's "Abominable Desolation" (its "New Mass" and "New Order") liturgizes this "new religion" as the cult of man. It pleases man–celebrates and serves man, as if man/woman were Christ.

To do so, latter-day Bishops jettisoned God's most precious gift and legacy–Christ's Mass. Posing themselves as if they were Christ's founding Apostles with power to change Christ's Church, the Bishops rejected and discarded the Catholic Mass and substituted "New Mass." The Bishops' "New Mass" firmly established itself in the confusing aftermath of Vatican Two, during the reign of Pope Paul VI.

[Therefore, in his inaugural encyclical, Pope John Paul II was able to assure us that "all are saved in Christ." Furthermore, his favorite misquote of St. Irenaeus became "The glory of God is man." This is apparent in his catechism which gives the impression that God fell in love with (sinful) man and could not resist becoming a man.]

The Apocalyptic Beasts (Apoc 13) are informed by the "spirit of Satan;" the Second Beast is 666–man enthroned. Paul VI liturgically enthroned man while Pope John Paul II perfected and set in stone, this enthronement of man. Genesis 3; Genesis 4 (describing the first "New Mass" of Cain); John 1; and Apocalypse 13 illustrate how the worship or cult of man comes from Satan. Apocalypse 13 describes both the New Age Government and the New Age "Church of Man" (6) glorified and honored as God, the "666 church." When Catholic faith and morals serve man, they serve Satan. The church itself becomes the Second Beast.

Following the dictum, "one believes what one prays," the Bishops' "New Mass" gradually dispelled Catholic belief and practice, distorting the worship that should be God's unto man. Christ's Church dwindles while the Bishops' "new religion" gains politically correct ascendance. The Bishops' Revolt,

with their new age "New Mass" has already succeeded within the Roman Rite.

Cardinal Ratzinger confessed that the traditional Latin or Roman Rite no longer exists. Thus, he confirms the brutally frank affirmation of this fact in 1976 by Fr. Joseph Gelineau, one of the most influential liturgists of his times.

> **"The Roman Rite as we knew it no longer exists. It has been destroyed."**
>
> **Fr. Joseph Gelineau, 1976**

> **"Today we might ask: 'Is there a Latin Rite at all any more?' Certainly, there is no awareness of it. To most people, the liturgy appears to be something for the individual congregation to arrange."**
>
> **Joseph Cardinal Ratzinger, 2003**

Within the ecclesial wing governed by the Bishops in Revolt, the Roman Rite Canonized Mass allegedly has been "overshadowed" by the present illicit imposition of the Bishops' "New Mass" replacing Holy Mass. "New Mass" defines the Bishops' "new religion," just as Christ's Canonized Mass defines the Catholic Church. While the Revolting Bishops' ears are itching to hear the song of the "fat lady singing," in spite of all efforts, the Canonized Latin Mass is not "over." The Canonized Latin Mass movement grows instead of dying.

Chapter Nineteen

"NEW MASS" LITURGIZES APOCALYPTIC APOSTASY (Apoc. 13)

High ranking church authorities devised a liturgical program to unite the establishment church in spirit and in truth with the Second Beast of the Apocalypse (Apoc 13). The existential church forced faithful Catholics to abandon the Catholic Religion; to conform to the new humanism, the cult of man. Addressing the United Nations, Pope Paul VI indicated his determination to so program the existential church. In closing Vatican II, he said:

> **"The religion of God made man [Christ's religion] has come up against the religion of man who makes himself God. And what happened?...in our new humanism: we also, we, more than anyone else, have the cult of man..." --Pope Paul VI, closing speech, Vatican Two, Dec. 1965, *Catholic Documents,* Jan. 1966**

Did you understand Pope Paul VI? He confessed that his "New Mass" worshiped man, not God: "We more that anyone else have the cult of man." Of course, he can't take all the credit. Pope John XXIII paved the way with his obsession to impose ecumenism, which betrayed and diminished Catholicism, as well as,

introduced the "new humanism" into the existential church. As Bishop of Rome, Paul VI joined the Bishops' Revolution, liturgically enthroning man when he acceded to and tolerated the "New Mass," the celebration of the cult of man. Pope John Paul II perfected this enthronement of man, this new religion rapidly replacing the Christ-given Catholic Religion. Within Catholicism, Christ is the Way. Within the apocalyptic apostate "new religion," man is the way:

> **"For the Church, all ways lead to Man...Man is the primary route that the Church must travel; he is the primary and fundamental way."**
> **PopeJohn Paul II, *Redemptor Hominis,* inaugural encyclical**

When Catholic faith and morals serve man, they serve Satan and the existential church becomes the Second Beast. In this process of devolution, the establishment church gradually rids itself of Catholic belief and practice, it being only a matter of time until the Christ-instituted Church completely gives way to the Bishops' apostate "new church." The apocalyptic "New Mass" is characterized by these (and other) specific New Order (Novus Ordo) new age qualities:

☛ **Worship and fear of God give way to relating to God as a doting grandfather, who is ever pleased with the doings of his beloved grandchildren.**

☛ **Divine Liturgy is radically transformed into new age humanism, wherein man praises himself (as god) and Christ is "remembered," but He is no longer Saviour. A false Christ made to image perfect man is feigned worship as the worshiping communities are programmed to hold that each person is as sinless as Holy Mary; ignoring, suppressing, her unique God-given role, her Immaculate Heart is blasphemed.**

☛ **The existential church is reduced to an ever-mutating creed, re-defined by the Bishops' "living tradition" (while Apostolic Tradition is denied). In their "self-bestowed divine rights," Bishops exercise power to mandate "New Mass."**

☛ **"New Mass" demonstrates that the existential church is no longer one, holy, catholic, apostolic.**

☛ **Using Vatican II as a vehicle to accomplish their "New Mass," Bishops usurped papal authority; refusing "obedience to" the Apostolic See, while demanding strict "obedience for" their "New Mass," "New Ordinal," "new religion," "new cult of sex," etc. elevating themselves, posing themselves, as if they were Christ's very own "living apostles" among us, with absolute, monarchical power.**

☛ These disobedient Revolting Bishops abolished Holy Ordered Priests and bestowed the priesthood upon all: "We all celebrate 'New Mass.'"

☛ The Bishops' "new religion" is now merely one of many organizations which work for self-realization of mankind and dedicates itself to evangelizing man's responsibility to the eco-system, based on his ever increasing awareness of his obligations which arise from his auto-divinization and the limitation of "religious concern" to this world (and to his "flesh," one might add).

☛ The Bible, the Mass and the catechism (as binding Catholic Faith and morals) are distorted into irrelevant guidelines or ways to define, please and inspire the new man, created in the imagined likeness of God, by the ever-changing directives of alleged "experts," as given to us by reigning, disobedient, malfeasant Bishops.

☛ Ecumenism as a dedicated betrayal of *extra ecclesiam nulla salus,* is directed toward the evolution or growth of the Second Beast of the Apocalypse, (in service to the First Beast) in the making of the best possible world– government of

man by human standards.

- ☛ **Love of God is reduced to love of man. Love of man, in turn, makes obsolete, useless and counter-productive, any love of God. "Intimacy with the Divine," characterizing the liturgical life of each Catholic, has been discarded and prohibited.**

- ☛ **Each is "as God," sinless; no longer need man as sinner plead to Christ for grace and mercy. Devotion to Christ (as the only Saviour from sin) is out. The Bishops' "communal celebrations" of the sin of presumption ("New Mass") is in.**

- ☛ **Basic supernaturals, such as sin, Hell, purgatory, judgment, Christ as Saviour, penance for sin, mortification of the flesh, etc. are unmentionables within the Bishops' "New Mass."**

- ☛ **Irenical obsession prevails. Peace must be attained at any cost; neither Pope nor Bishop provides any justification for war. As pure pacifists, post-Vatican II popes, clergy and laity have become allies and enablers for a new world dictatorship.**

"New Mass" Words of Consecration Express Apocalyptic Apostasy

Why were the words of Consecration mistranslated– even from the "Latin New Mass Standard?" *"Pro multis"* does not mean "for all." The Bishops' "New Mass," prays fundamental belief in the salvation of all, forcing the consecration prayers into satanic sacrilege. Their "New Mass" rejects any and all need of "special salvation" by Christ, since "in Christ, all have been saved automatically, by being born."

"New Mass" Third Eucharistic Prayer Celebrates Presumption & Expresses Apostasy

The "New Mass" prays that man may be united to fellow man: *"In mercy and love, unite all your children wherever they may be."* In fact, the God of Biblical Revelation is the Great Separator, Whose final act vis a vis mankind is to separate (not unite) His Hell-destined children from His Elect. So who is "this God" to whom the Bishops' "New Mass" prays for the union of all humans? To avoid blatant heresy and apostasy, "wherever they may be" must, at least,

be replaced with "whatever this might mean." However, within the apostate "New Mass" matrix, existential churchmen firmly believe in and boldly pray universal salvation. There is no need to pray for salvation; no need for Holy Mass! Therefore, the apostate "New Mass" prayers must express presumption and conviction of universal salvation.

"New Mass" 1st Eucharistic Prayer in Masses for Children Expresses Apostasy

---

"New Mass" 1st Eucharistic Prayer in Masses for Children

"In the preface of this liturgy, we pray:
God our Father, you have brought us here together so that we can give you thanks and praise for all that is beautiful in the world and for the happiness you have given us. We praise you for daylight and for your earth and for all the people who live on it, and for our life which comes from you. We know that you are good. You love us and do great things for us . So we all say together: Holy, Holy Holy..."

In "New Mass," the children do not thank and praise God for salvation, God's greatest gift. Why don't these children praise and thank God for salvation?

Obviously, they believe in Apocalyptic "universal presumption." Within the "New Mass," all are already saved; thus, there is no need to burden children with the necessity of salvation. Christ as Saviour is rendered meaningless. Working and praying for the salvation of one's soul is alien and discomforting, since, in "New Mass," souls are dedicated to making life better on earth, sinfully presuming that all are saved from Hell.

"New Mass" 4th Eucharistic Prayer
Apostasy of Presumption and Universal Salvation

Among the legion of apostate liturgies in the Bishops' "New Mass," this prayer serves to indoctrinate "the hesitant" into being convinced of salvation and ever rejoicing in the sin of presumption, even salvation of all. As it stands, this prayer assures the congregation that God has led all to find Him and all will be saved. Therefore, no man need seek salvation, nor be a Catholic, nor attend the Holy Sacrifice of the Mass. Similarly, a later prayer boldly states that this "sacrifice" brings salvation to the whole world.

Apostasy In Some "New Mass" Prefaces

☛ **The Easter II preface states: "His (Christ's) resurrecting is our rising to life..." Should this prayer not say "His resurrection is our *pledge of rising to life?"* No! Man as god must rise to life. In truth, salvation from Hell is God's freely bestowed gift, not any man's "choice." Only the Elect, as God's chosen, will rise to "eternal life."**

☛ **In the 4th Preface for Sundays in Ordinary Times, "New Mass" prays: "In his return to you in glory, we enter into your heavenly kingdom." The "New Mass" prays consummate demonic pride.**

☛ **In the Christmas Preface II, "New Mass" prays: "Today, man has become one again with God." More accurately, especially, for contemporary man, it should read: "Today, each of us is given the great opportunity to become one again with God." Presumption is a capital sin in the Catholic Church. "New Mass," prays presumption as virtue.**

☛ **In Easter IV preface, instead of "A broken world has been renewed," "New Mass" should (if Catholic) pray " Teach us, O God, to despise this** world and to seek to attain Heavenly goals." Instead, man and "man's world" is now renewed and godlike; and is in process of being ever more renewed and even more godlike by man's own efforts--according to the "New Mass" liturgy. "New Mass" liturgizes apocalyptic apostasy within. "New Mass" had to reject the "Last Gospel" (Jn 1) since this liturgy prays as to believe in, serve and "worship" the world and the flesh.

Apostasy In Newchurch Funerals

In services for the dead, "New Mass" does not pray for deliverance from Hell, as if the very idea of the danger of Hell is absurd. The living are already sainted because "man is god," according to the satanic faith of "New Mass!" Unencumbered men are here on earth to love each other and the earth itself. (Such is the nature of the apocalyptic apostasy celebrated in the Bishops' "New Mass" funerals.)

☛ The "New Mass" 1st Christian Death Preface prays: "Lord, for your faithful people, life is changed, not ended. When the body of our earthly dwelling lies in death, "'we' gain an

everlasting dwelling place in Heaven." Now, to be Catholic and not apostate and thus invalid, if "we" is intended to refer to "your faithful people," then it should not be used. Instead, "they" must be used. Who, then are "we?" Obviously, within the apocalyptic apostasy, "we" are "man– individually and collectively; "we" are gods. In reality of Catholic substance, such communal praying is "praying presumption."

☛ **Later, in the Special Remembrance,** (E.P. III) **"New Mass" prays: "There (in Heaven) we shall see you, our God, as you are. We shall become like you and praise you forever." Is presumption sin still sin? Yes, except, of course, for those who, satanically deceived, now believe in and pray "New Mass" Novus Ordo. Why not pray "We hope to see you as you are" instead of "We shall see you as you are?" Why not pray: "We hope to become like you" instead of "We shall become like you," meaning that "We presume to be saved." "New Mass" prays that man is god. As god, he is self-sufficient. He is "saved." He no longer needs to pray for salvation. "Hope" becomes sin. Presumption becomes satanic virtue. According to the preponderance of evidence, the Bishops' "New Mass" is conclusively not valid, since their religion is satanic. Q.E.D.**

☛ **"New Mass" prays (the sin of presumption) that faith may so increase as to allow all to believe that N. __ the deceased, is in Heaven: "Merciful Lord... open the gates of paradise to your servant and help us to comfort one another with assurance of faith until we all meet in Christ and are with you and our brother/sister forever."** (p.103, Order of Christian Funerals, ICEL).

Work up a belief in presumption (a cardinal demonic sin). If you have enough "presumption," rest assured that those who were our friends will be our friends forever. Cultivate presumption!Believe that the ties of friendship made here on earth will exist forever and ever. So, if you had robber-friends, prostitute friends, or any kind of friends, be comforted. These ties will endure forever presuming that, man as he is, is god.

The saddest realization is that "New Mass" prays for man to love only himself. He no longer cares about the spiritual harm (and even death) he is inflicting upon the innocent and vulnerable. Indeed, as Jesus predicted, the love of many has grown cold, ice cold (Mt 24:12). **The love of many "freezes" God's life out of children and enkindles Satan's lies in their hearts.**

How can any Bishop stand by and let children be

deprived of the right to Mass Prayers which clearly and convincingly express the Catholic Faith? How can any Bishop allow prayers to become vehicles for "praying presumption" and believing into the heresy of universal salvation? What Jesus speculated as impossible–that a father would give his child a stone to eat and a poisonous snake with which to play–has materialized. "New Mass" clergy do both of these "impossibilities" unto the eternal damnation of their victims.

Recall the "New Mass" funerals you attend. Was not the deceased "sent to Heaven" in most, if not all, cases? Binding and official Church teaching requires that, unless the preacher had a very special revelation from God that the deceased was in Heaven, the preacher was subject to severe censure if he placed the deceased automatically in Heaven. Specifically, the dogmatic Council of Trent condemns such popes, bishops, priests, deacons, etc. who do so.

Which pope and council overruled the Council of Trent so that it is no longer binding? Perhaps, one should ask: "Which disobedient, latter-day Bishop (who thinks he is a "living" apostle) overruled the Council of Trent? Answer: All of them?

Heretical Tenor of "New Mass"

The heretical tenor of "New Mass" can be demonstrated by citing a personal experience. I, myself, was once forbidden by my Bishop to preach at funerals because I denied one heresy expressed in "New Mass"– that each of us certainly goes to Heaven.

I dared to express the true Catholic doctrine concerning Purgatory, Hell, the need for prayer for the deceased and the Catholic Dogma concerning the ordinary uncertainty that any particular person is definitely in Heaven. After I was reprimanded for mentioning "Hell" in funeral sermons, I soon figured out how to cope.

After being reinstated to say funeral "Masses," I employed a "Jesuitical trick" (having been educated and ordained as a Jesuit). I changed the initial oration or prayer to have it reflect Catholic truth (e.g."We pray that N.__ may in God's mercy avoid Hell and be destined for eternal joy in Heaven").

Since then, I no longer had any trouble with my funeral preaching. My Jesuitical solution also demonstrates that what one leads one's flock to pray, one's flock is led to accept and believe. Of course, all of this happened before my full conversion to Christ's Holy Sacrifce of the Canonized Latin Mass, before my return to Catholicism.

Fr. Paul Trinchard

Et Cetera

What has been presented in this chapter is merely a sampling of the prepondernce of evidence which conclusively proves that "New Mass" is "null and void," to use the words of Pope Leo XIII in *Apostolicae Curae.* The Orations and other Versicles have not been considered. However, they consist of the same heretical "New Age" (Novus Ordo) mindset. The form of "New Mass," being *all of the words used to pray "New Mass,"* constitutes or "determines" invalidity. The religion "in and from" these words is alien to Catholicism.

By Way of Stark Contrast:
The Canonized Latin Mass Prayers

"The holy canon is so free from error that it contains nothing that does not in the highest degree savour of holiness and piety."
Council of Trent, Sess 22

Instituted by Christ and canonized by Pope Saint Pius V and Trent, the Canonized Latin Mass does not teach universal salvation. The "atmosphere" or "geist" of the Canonized Mass ritual is a clear and

convincing didactic reinforcement of pertinent "God-affirming, man-humbling" Catholic dogma and teaching regarding:

- **our own personal uncertainty of salvation;**
- **the need to pray to God, Our Lady and the saints for the graces to be saved, praying to become holy that we may eternally abide with them;**
- **our necessity to die daily with Christ or to be crucified with Christ–by God's graces;**
- **our desperate and pressing need for God's graces–as obtained by attending or saying Mass and other prayers to avoid Mortal Sin, to persevere to the end;**
- **our and others' need for prayers–especially, "Mass prayers"–to lessen the pains of Purgatory;**
- **our and others' need for Mass and other essentially Catholic "Prayer Dogmas" to avoid going to Hell.**

Chapter Twenty

WHERE IS THE CHURCH (AS IN "EXTRA ECCLESIAM, NULLA SALUS")?

St. Athanasius, to whom it was objected:
"You have all the bishops against you," answered with faith:
"That proves that they are all against the Church."

It is far easier to clarify the notion of "validity" and apply it to the present than it is to clarify "church" and apply it to the present. Living in the very worst existential church in history (a "new church" with a "new religion" produced by the Bishops' Revolt), we suffer liturgical (and fiducial) apostasy within the ecclesial church establishment, as well as, "without" or outside of the Church. To define, or more importantly, to know "how" to "join" and remain faithful to the only Church outside of which there is no salvation, is the crucial contemporary problem facing sincere salvation-seeking faithful Catholics.

The Council of Trent gives Catholics their starting point. It defines the Sacrament of Baptism. Then, it dogmatizes the necessity to be baptized in order to be saved. One becomes a Catholic (as in *extra ecclesiam*

nulla salus) **by the Sacrament of Baptism. One is cut off from full governmental union with the existential church by (material or formal) schism.**

The most difficult task facing Catholics today is to find and attend a valid Mass without becoming heretical– without embracing heresy. The very Heart of Christ's Church is the New and Eternal Testament, the Holy Sacrifice of Mass celebrated by Holy Ordered Priests as successors of the Apostles, as Christ and His Church irrevocably decreed.

Must one go to the Orthodox to find this? Must one go to a valid priest without faculties from Rome? Must one go to a retired Catholic Holy Ordered priest?

After finding a place to go for Holy Mass, keep in mind that one is cut off from the life of Christ and His Church by heresy (the deliberate personal denial in thought, word and deed of what one must believe or do to be a faithful Catholic). Beware of liturgical heresy (by participating in an invalid "New Mass," as if it were a Mass). Such an heretical deed constitutes an act of apostasy. One Bishop who "repented of the Bishops' "New Mass," the late Bishop Lazo of the Philippines, once noted:

You will perhaps ask me the question "Why did you become a traditional Catholic?" Well, it is this: I became one because I rejected the "New Mass"...

"Why did you reject the "New Mass?" I reject the "New Mass" for many reasons. First of all, when the Conciliar bishops were reforming the liturgy, the Masons had in mind that the light of Faith had to be extinguished. The Holy Mass must be snuffed out...But the people are addicted, they love the Mass so much!

"What did they do to deceive the people?" They removed the Mass but they gave a substitute; and the substitute is called the Novus Ordo. That is why we hear in the Phillipines sometime, "The "New Mass" [Novus Ordo] is the bogus Catholic Mass. It is a fake."

That is what the people say! That comes from the people! Those who don't blindly trust and obey their bishops have educated themselves and have come to the conclusion that this is not real Mass. It is a meal, a narrative, a memorial.

Bishop Lazo, *Catholic Family News,* quoted 1998

Bishop Lazo referred to the fact that Vatican II was hijacked within a week after it convened (by the Suenens "Rhine faction") the years-long preparatory work of a thousand scholars scuttled. The Masonic anti-Christ and anti-Church intellectuals came in and wrote Vatican II to their own liking as an ambiguous platform statement which established the mechanism for creating and subsequently, ruthlessly

imposing, "New Mass," which is a Masonic and new age compatible service.

The Canonized Mass (Eastern or Latin) is the very Heart of Catholicism. How can one settle for a church body which in practice rejects its Heart? How can such a body give sufficient life (graces to live so as to attain Heaven)? Note that within the Roman Patriarchate, unless "the Marian Remnant" (Apoc 12) prevails, Catholics will be forced to live without Holy Mass. Our Lady of Fatima reflected on our dire condition:. "In the end, all you with have left is the Rosary and [thereby] devotion to my Immaculate Heart." Only the "specially blessed" will have the Mass.

Bishops have liturgically apostatized. Their "New Mass" is not a Mass. The Sacred Heart has departed from "New Mass." Since God deemed it necessary to give the Fatima message, it is fitting to acknowledge that it must have concerned the absence of Christ's Holy Mass.

"Build a Chapel Here!"
Our Lady in her apparitions.

[Our Lady, in all of her Church-approved apparitions, requests that a chapel be built for Christ's Canonized Mass.]

"That is why right now, build altars in your own homes, and invite priests to come there and offer the Sacrifice of the Mass!

...Let there be a modern version of the catacombs! It is better to have the real Mass on an altar in your home than a phony, community service in what used to be Catholic churches. ..

Because the days are over for speeches; the days are over for publications; the days are over for pamphlets; the days of action are here!

We must have nothing less than the presence of God among us!"
Rev. Dr. Gommar de Pauw, *Conciliar or Catholic?* 1967, www.traditio.com/tradlib'depauw67.txt

Prophecy Fulfilled

Today we have the exact carbon copy of the situation St. Pius X described in 1903, where he made it clear that the promoters of error today are not found among our declared enemies –the promoters of error today are found in the very ranks of our own Church! Today we are witnessing that exact situation.

We are also witnessing the very thing which was predicted in Fatima in 1917. And I could see right up, it's not exactly making that public. But I don't pretend to have the text of that message of Our Blessed Mother in Fatima, but the text I received in Rome has a few paragraphs there which are still very much of interest. It was predicted then and it is happening now.

"A time of severe trial is coming for the Church. Not today, nor tomorrow," the Blessed Mother said in 1917, "but in the second half of the 20th century. Humanity will not develop as God desires it. Mankind will become sacrilegious and trample underfoot the gift it has received. No longer will order reign anywhere. "Even in the high places," the Blessed Mother predicted, "Satan will reign and direct the course of things. He will even succeed in infiltrating into the highest positions in the Church. Cardinals will oppose cardinals and bishops will oppose bishops. Satan will enter into their very midst. The Church will be obscured and all the world will be thrown into confusion." Rev. Dr. Gommar de Pauw, *Conciliar or Catholic?*

Chapter Twenty-One

SNAKES, BARKING DOGS & THE REST OF US

> **"Those who sit in a house of which the use is forgotten: are like snakes that lie on mouldering stairs, content in the sunlight. And others run about like dogs, full of enterprise, sniffing and barking....These are not justified, nor the others."**
>
> ***The Rock,* T.S.Eliot**

There are three types of people "within" the existential church:bishops, priests and people, who, like unto serpents, are content with "New Mass;" annoying and ineffective dogs (those who dislike the "New Mass," yet refuse to hold that the "New Mass" is conclusively invalid); and Catholics who are exclusively devoted to the Canonized Latin Mass as the one and only Mass Ritual of and for the Latin Rite; and who, thereby, are led to perceive the "New Mass" as conclusively invalid. These are the Marian end times prophets. (MAETA "means" MArian End Times Apostolate.)

One is familiar with those who lie among the ruins of Christ's Church "content in the sunlight." One is

familiar with the serpents. They contentedly and peacefully dwell in the house whose purpose was at first denied and by now is largely forgotten. One is familiar with the barking dogs. They constitute the majority of "New Mass" (who accept that "Novus Ordo is valid") "trads."

Such barking dogs are upset with the liturgical problem, but fail to analyze it correctly and fail to embrace the only right solution. Barking dogs vehemently and ineffectively object to the "New Mass" for emotional or "substantially irrelevant" reasons. They fail to ascertain and object to the invalidity of the "New Mass."

Therefore, their efforts are as barking dogs: as meaningless as the "New Mass" which "mentions the word, 'sacrifice,'" but does not accomplish the Sacrifice of Calvary "in an unbloody manner;" does not offer Christ-Immaculate Victim; and, therefore, does not produce Christ-Sacrament. One finds it remarkable that the words of Cardinal Manning, second Archbishop of Westminster, apply today:

> "Where the Blessed Sacrament is not, all dies. As when the sun departs all things sicken and decay, and when life is gone the body returns to dust; so with any province or member of the Church...

A change which held both on earth and in heaven had been accomplished...There was no Holy Sacrifice offered morning by morning. The Scriptures were read, but there was no Divine Teacher to interpret them. The Magnificat was chanted still, but it rolled along the empty roofs, for Jesus was no longer on the altar. So it is to this day. There is no light, no tabernacle, no altar, nor can be, till Jesus shall return thither. They stand like the open sepulcher, and we may believe that angels are there, ever saying, 'He is not here. Come and see the place where the Lord was laid....'" – Cardinal Henry Edward Manning, † 1892.

The Blessed Sacrament, Centre of Immutable Truth

Where the Mass Liturgy as instituted by Christ is not celebrated by a "Holy Ordered Priest," there cannot exist the Holy Sacrifice and the Blessed Sacrament. Such a "mass" is devoid of life. Such are the Anglican Service and the Bishops' "New Mass."

Protecting Catholic Substance

"How will you escape eternal damnation if you neglect or worse yet, distort so Great Salvation, the Mass?"

A paraphrase of Heb 2:3

This Pauline question should haunt the bishops and

priests, as well as Protestants. Paul Tillich clarified the priestly function and the notion of "Catholic Substance." Priests are here to preserve, "apply intact," and hand on intact, the Catholic Substance– that which makes the Catholic Church be Christ's Church (i.e. for our concern as Latin Rite Catholics, the forever fixed, in words and gestures, Canonized Latin Rite Mass).

The Canonized Latin Mass is the Mass Text from Apostolic Times which, in the Latin Rite, constitutes or "brings about" the living Heart of the Catholic Substance. Christ gave His apostles the "exact formula" to effect the most Holy Mass, the Living Testament in Christ's Salutary Blood. Christ entrusted this sacred formula to His Holy Ordered Priests in each generation of the existential church's history (to be "applied" as given by Christ and passed on intact).

Call for Prophets

Prophets, according to Paul Tillich, are here to correct priestly failures in times of gross priestly failure. Prophets grieve for the broken Church, the Church without its Temple.They grieve “to and with” the Sacred Heart and the Immaculate Heart. They plead with the King to bring back the Temple–Christ’s Holy Sacrifice and Holy Sacrament. God answers. He sends ever more Marian prophets to restore Holy Mass to Jerusalem, to His existential church (cf. Apoc 12).

Marian prophets are sent by God to rebuild the Temple; to work with the sword in one hand and a trowel in the other. They must fend off snakes and barking dogs as they “rebuild” the Church.

There are those who build the Temple.
And those who prefer that the Temple should not be built.
In the days of Nehemiah the Prophet
There was no exception to the general rule.

Nehemiah grieved for the broken city, Jerusalem;
And the King gave him leave to depart
That he might rebuild the Temple
So he went, with a few, to Jerusalem.

Jerusalem lay waste, consumed with fire;
No place for a beast to pass.
There were enemies without to destroy him,
And spies and self-seekers within,

When he and his men laid their hands to rebuilding,
They built as men must build
With the sword in one hand and the trowel in the other.

T. S. Eliot

Theologically Speaking

The Holy Mass, because it is instituted by Christ, is never to be changed. Theologians agree that the Canon of the Mass from *"Suscipe sancte Pater..."* through the *"Per Ipsum..."* cannot be changed. To be the Mass, the Mass must be as it was in Apostolic Tradition.

The Canonized Latin Mass Text is perfect theology. However, as such, it was never taught in the seminaries or in other classes. My books (Mystery of Faith and Latin Mass Prayers Explained) present the minimum "prayerful knowledge" of the Mass of which every Catholic should be aware. The existential church's way back to Catholicism is to come to appreciate "its priceless possession," Christ's Canonized Latin Mass Text; to pray Christ's Holy Canonized Latin Mass Text; and to live Christ's Canonized Latin Mass prayers.

Fr. Paul Trinchard

Christ's Living Will and Testament for His Church

The Holy Mass is Christ's Salutary Deed–His Living Will and Testament for His Church. The Holy Mass is the Will of the Father, the accomplished Salutary Deed of Christ in a bloody manner once and forever at Calvary, and, as promised by Christ, graced by the Salutary Action of the Holy Ghost in an unbloody manner in perpetuity, as instructed by Christ to His Apostles; and thus, cannot be changed by any man. Christ instructed His Apostles in the manner in which this Salutary Deed was to be made present in perpetuity through His Holy Ordered Priests in an unbloody manner. End of story -- no Pope; no Bishop; can override God's Will, nor any Priest.

How dare the Bishops change Christ's "Living Will and Testament for His Church? Pope Leo XIII, honoring St. Joseph as Patron of the Church, refused to add St. Joseph to the Canon indicating that he was merely the Pope (and not Christ) and, thus, could not do so. Earlier popes also refused any change to the Canon. This is the Apostolic Tradition of the Church in action– preserving Christ's Will and Testament!

The Most Holy Mass, man's salutary necessity and God's Greatest Gift, as Christ's Salutary Deed (past and forever completed tense) can never be changed. The Mass must be as Christ accomplished His Salutary Deed; and as He instructed to be re-accomplished by His Apostles and Holy Ordered Priests in an unbloody manner. The Mass must be as it always was, as Christ's Will and Testament decreed, as His Church canonized and as it is in Heaven: or, there is NO Mass!

Other Works by Fr. Trinchard

Apostasy Within

God's Word

Pray the Holy Mass

New Mass In Light of the Old

New Age New Mass

All About Salvation

The Awesome Fatima Consecrations

The Abbot & Me On Liturgy

The Mystery of Faith

Fatima Apocalypse Now

Latin Mass Prayers Explained